Behind the Gold Curtain

THE STORY OF THE METROPOLITAN OPERA: 1883-1950

By Mary Ellis Peltz

Sponsored by the
Metropolitan Opera Guild, Inc.
New York

Farrar Straus and Company, New York

Book designed by Nelson Gruppo.

Type set by Atlantic Typographers, New York.

Printed by The Murray Printing Company, Wakefield, Mass.

Bound by H. Wolff, New York.

PICTURE CREDITS.

Abresch—73, 83; Acme—41; Apeda—73; DeGueldre—41, 51;
DuPont—12, 13, 19, 27, 32, 35, 41; Edwards—53; Elvira—32; Falk—12, 21, 28;
Farr—92; Feinberg—27; Frissell—86; Georg—36; Greenhaus—89; Gubelman—7;
Healy Coll.—6, 10; Keystone—83, 95; Mapleson—91; McCook coll.—42;
Melancon—4, 15, 66, 85, 88; Mishkin—36, 41, 54, 55; More—18; Morton—53;
Piver—73; Pittner—83; Reutlinger—28; Schafer—79; Steichen—13;
Toppo—13; Tracy—59; Valente—79; Villani—51;
Sudak—47; Times—53, 54, 55, 59, 64, 65, 66, 68, 71, 74, 75, 76, 77, 79, 80, 82;

Foreword

WHEN THE great gold curtain parts on the Metropolitan Opera stage a new world lies open to the imagination. Behind this curtain may stand ancient Thebes, or eighteenth-century Paris, medieval Antwerp or a starlit terrace in Nagasaki. In the ever-ever land of opera the years take little toll. Time and space are alike eradicated by the magic of art.

For sixty-seven years this miracle has been accomplished in our beloved Opera House. On the stage, artists who made its fame have come and gone. In the auditorium, generations of opera-lovers have watched the curtain rise. Traditions have been handed down on both sides of the footlights. Novelties have shocked the audience and later mellowed into tradition.

The story of Metropolitan Opera is a long one, a saga which merits many tellings and which is read with eager interest by succeeding generations. From time to time our Opera Guild has revealed new aspects of this operatic cavalcade. Six years ago we published a small book, *Metropolitan Opera Milestones*, which outlined the developments of the theatre itself and the most outstanding events of its first sixty years. Now at the close of the regime of Edward Johnson, it is fitting that the Metropolitan story should be reviewed and brought up to date. Fascinating old pictures have been discovered. New photographs have been made possible by special lighting and the use of modern lenses.

No attempt has been made to cover all the distinguished names in the roster or all the important operas in the repertory. Our author has condensed some of the colorful facts in the great pageant that has swept the stage, and illumined the pages with a variety of illustrations.

Music, alas, is lacking, but that, perhaps, will echo from the memory, as we recall the thrilling moments in Metropolitan Opera history which are here set forth. To those of us who have been privileged to hear opera in the historic theatre, the very names of the great artists are music. To the vast radio audience music seems to emanate from the air itself.

So let us conclude this brief overture with a warm welcome to our Opera House, a toast to its glorious past, a salute to its magnificent future. And now, up with the curtain!

MRS. AUGUST BELMONT

Contents ★ ★ ★

★ ★ ★

The Metropolitan proscenium as it looks today.

The Opera House on January 2, 1884, when a ball was given for the Nursery and Child's Hospital. At midnight "the lanciers" were danced and supper was served in the adjacent unfinished apartment building dining-rooms.

The Metropolitan in 1884, when horsecars served Broadway. Next year the city removed the telegraph wires and poles.

"A Noble House"

THE METROPOLITAN OPERA HOUSE of today is quite a different building from the theatre which was opened on October 22, 1883. True, the yellow brick walls rise as sturdily as ever from the trapezoid block bounded by Broadway and Seventh Avenue, Thirty-ninth and Fortieth streets, testifying to the economy of the architect, Josiah Cleaveland Cady, who wasted no penny on ostentatious decoration of the $1,732,478.71 which was the cost of the building and the site. Today, however, streamlined shop windows invade the "early Italian Renaissance" façade, with its round arched Romanesque panels, Two roof stages add to the bulk of the original Seventh Avenue edifice.

The importance of these outer changes shrinks in comparison with the developments of the interior. Though music is the most ethereal of the arts, opera responds to the fashions of the day with the sensitiveness of quicksilver. Even the brick and stone of an opera house must yield with the flexibility of public taste. And thus it has been with the Metropolitan.

From the beginning the process of expansion was evident. New York society had outgrown the nine Parterre Boxes available at the Academy of Music, where grand opera had been presented from 1854. The new fortunes of railroads, banks and real estate stood ready to support the arts.

When the progressive citizen George Henry Warren visited August Belmont, president of the Academy Board of Directors, on April 3, 1880, he was not im-

7

pressed by the suggested compromise of twenty-six additional boxes in the Fourteenth Street theatre. Mr. Warren's vision could see further still. He returned to his colleagues Robert Goelet and George Griswold Haven and on April 7 informed the New York *Times* that $600,000 had already been subscribed to purchase a site and build an adequate opera house. On the historic opening night of the Metropolitan, no less than 122 boxes were filled.

The choice of the architect was in itself democratic. Four firms were invited to enter the competition: G. E. Harvey, George B. Post, Potter and Harrison and J. Cleaveland Cady. Each was paid a $3000 retainer fee and given three months to submit a design. On October 15, 1880, Mr. Cady's appointment was announced.

The purchase of the Broadway location was confirmed on March 15, 1881, but difficulties with leaseholders and rising building costs delayed the work to such an extent that a year later only the foundation had been completed. As late as March 27, 1882, the original plans were further modified to provide additional revenue. It was decided to fill the corners of the building with rent-bearing apartments.

On May 24, 1883, the new opera house was put to its first official use: a meeting at which 70 boxes of the two lower tiers were drawn by lot among the 65 stockholders. (Messrs George Peabody Wetmore, George Henry Warren, William K. Vanderbilt, Robert and Ogden Goelet undertook the responsibility of two boxes apiece.) The first president of the Metropolitan Opera-house Company, Ltd., J. N. A. Griswold, does not appear to have reserved a box, although his successor, James A. Roosevelt, drew number 55 on the second tier.

The choice of J. Cleaveland Cady for architect seems to have been entirely due to his efforts in the competition. Born and brought up in Providence, R. I., an ardent Sunday-school teacher and amateur organist, this gentleman, it is stated by his nephew, William W. Ellsworth, "had never been to Europe, never seen one of the world's great opera houses, never attended a performance in his life." His professional renown was based largely on ecclesiastical and academic achievements. He was responsible for the main building of the Museum of Natural History, the Gallatin Bank, the old Presbyterian Hospital and many college edifices at Yale, Williams and elsewhere.

For European experience and a knowledge of operatic tradition, Mr. Cady seems to have relied on a twenty-four-year-old engineer and draftsman, Louis de Coppet Bergh, who was so encouraged when his firm was awarded the contract that he promptly married his fiancée and hurried away to a honeymoon on Lake Mohonk. The young man is said to have been indispensable to his employer, for Mr. Cady was forced to send three urgent telegrams to bring him back to his drafting board. His contribution to the opera house was recognized only after its completion, when his name was added to the title of the firm, but the building contained an anonymous memorial to his marriage. Before the theatre was finished, his infant son had died, and Bergh paid tribute to his memory by having the child's features appear as one of the cherubs which decorate the pilasters.

Five important considerations seem to have occupied the architects of the Metropolitan Opera House: a commodious auditorium, with ample boxes to provide for the growing ranks of New York society, good visibility and acoustics, an adequate stage and the elimination of fire hazards.

The original seating capacity compared to existing conditions follows:

SEATING, 1883			SEATING, 1950	
Parquet	600		Orchestra	713
12 Baignoire boxes	72		Orchestra circle	315
37 Parterre boxes	216		35 Parterre boxes	280
37 1st tier boxes	222		Grand tier, including Club and Guild boxes	288
36 2nd tier boxes	222		Dress circle	516
Balcony	735		Balcony	647
Gallery	978		Family circle	706
Total	3,045		Total	3,465

In order to secure good visibility, some 700 drawings were made of sight-lines from every part of the house to the sides and rear of the stage. Although the horseshoe type of auditorium which was in vogue through the eighteenth and nineteenth centuries precluded the perfect visibility of the modern theatres, with the steel construction of their large balconies, it is interesting to note the enthusiasm of Montgomery Schuyler, a contemporary writer in *Harper's Monthly.*

"It is safe to say that there is no theatre in which there are fewer bad seats in proportion to its size, nor any opera house in which the difference between the best and the worst boxes is so small."

The acoustics were enhanced by the generous use of wood in facing the auditorium and by an egg-shaped sound chamber of masonry underneath the orchestra pit.

The stage itself drew wondering comment for its brick work, 125 feet high and 106 feet wide, roofed with a clear span supported by an iron truss which was set upon rollers to provide for expansion and contraction.

The disastrous fire of the Ringtheater in Vienna in December, 1881 and many similar tragic episodes in the theatrical history of New York loomed large in the minds of the Metropolitan architects. The house was to be completely fireproof. Tiles, iron beams and brick arches composed the flooring, with the masonry exposed in the corridors. The ceiling of the auditorium was of iron. The ornamental work on the proscenium, decorated with Francis Lathrop's painting of Apollo and the Muses and flanked by Francis Maynard's figures of the Ballet and the Chorus, were all of metal. The stage was supported by a complex system of four thousand metal pieces. A large skylight was weighted to fall open in case of fire and prevent any blaze from mushrooming, while a network of pipes, fused with soft solder, offered elementary sprinkler protection from a large water tank. A fireproof screen hung next the dark blue plush curtain at the front of the stage. Although the theatre was lit by gas, wires were laid for electricity which had not yet been introduced throughout the city. Abundant staircases and exits permitted the house to be emptied in three minutes.

The decoration was entrusted to E. P. Treadwell, a Boston architect who was instructed by Mr. Cady to "avoid all tawdriness or garish display." The theatre was accordingly carpeted in rich red; the boxes were draped with curtains of old gold, bearing a pattern of slightly darker shade with dark red threads. Ivory was the prevailing tint for the woodwork and ceiling, although the box fronts were gilded and the walls were tinted pinkish orange.

From the earliest changes which were effected at the opera house after a single season the democratic trend was again evident. First, ample boxes for new fortunes; next, additional seats for the middle-priced clients.

In 1884 the second tier (actually third tier) boxes were eliminated and the space rearranged to form what is now the dress circle. The *Tribune* of November 18, 1884, also refers to "the wealth of new decorations" which adorned the theatre.

FIRE AND RECONSTRUCTION

During the seven seasons of opera in German, initiated by Leopold Damrosch with the support of the directors of the Metropolitan Opera-house Company, and continued after his death under the direction of the Secretary of the Board,

Loge staged a show on August 27, 1892, when the public crowded 7th Avenue to watch.

Edmund C. Stanton, we have no record of alterations in the structure of the opera house, nor in the single Italian season which followed them under the management of Abbey, Schoeffel and Grau. The disastrous fire which burned out the stage and seriously disfigured the auditorium on the morning of August 27, 1892, however, necessitated a radical reconstruction.

Confidence in Mr. Cady's original fire prevention installations may have accounted for the low insurance ($60,000) which had been placed on the opera house, but it was not sufficiently emphatic to keep the devices in use. The metal supports beneath the stage had impeded the technicians and been replaced by wood. In freezing weather it cost money to heat the tank which fed the sprinkler system, so the manager had emptied it. The fireproof curtain proved cumbersome and was chained up out of the way.

Having unconsciously "set the stage" for a conflagration, the Abbey, Schoeffel and Grau management proceeded to use the hazardous space to paint scenery for other theatres under the same direction. A workman's cigarette did the rest.

The cost of reconstruction was estimated at $300,000, but on September 26, 1892, it was announced that the Metropolitan Opera-house Co., Ltd., would not undertake the rebuilding. Nineteen of the original stockholders helped to form a new corporation, the Metropolitan Opera and Real Estate Company; sixteen new names were added and each of the thirty-five sponsors subscribed to three hundred shares of stock at $100 a share, for which he was awarded a Parterre box and a 35th interest in the property. In addition, each stockholder purchased $30,000 worth of bonds to reconstruct the theatre. With the funds thus provided the building was purchased at foreclosure proceedings and reconstruction was begun on April 14, 1893.

The audience which celebrated the reopening of the Metropolitan Opera House on November 27, 1893, witnessed major improvements. The baignoire boxes had been removed and replaced by 350 orchestra circle seats as well as improved standing room. An omnibus box on the south side of the grand tier broke the serried ranks of the second row of boxes. Both stage and parquet were lowered three feet to eliminate the sharp upward slope that had led into the auditorium from the foyer. Ten thousand electric lamps cast their radiance on the new red and gold Cheney silks which decorated the house.

CHANGES UNDER CONRIED

The extensive theatrical experience of Heinrich Conried, who took over the management of the Metropolitan in 1903, accounted for several of the alterations which increased the facilities of the opera house ten years later.

Under the supervision of Carl Lautenschläger of Munich, the stage was modernized. A new mechanical system of counterbalances relieved the stage hands in the manipulation of flies, drops and borders. A new stage floor permitted the sudden transformations necessary in the production of *Parsifal*. A new proscenium arch was designed by the architectural firm of Carrère and Hastings.

The public which attended Caruso's debut on November 23, 1903, also en-

Metropolitan Managers

Henry Abbey lost half a million in 1883-84 but did much better in the 1890's.

Walter Damrosch and his father Leopold, both pioneers for Richard Wagner.

Edmund C. Stanton, the urbane Secretary of the Metropolitan directorate.

Opera stars were good business to Maurice Grau, who knew human nature well.

Héinrich Conried, professional showman, who introduced Parsifal.

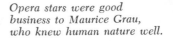

12

joyed the new smoking room and foyer on the grand tier, returned refreshed to the new chairs in the auditorium to admire the deep maroon draperies, silks and carpets which had been provided by the house of W. & J. Sloane.

A radical change in the management also became apparent when Mr. Conried undertook the operatic helm. Under the leadership of James Hazen Hyde and Henry Rogers Winthrop, a new producing company was formed with each director taking $10,000 of stock. For the first time the theatre was leased by the real estate company not to a private individual, but to an organization bearing the name of the Metropolitan — the Conried Metropolitan Opera Company.

In November, 1905, new curtains of figured gold damask won the approval of the opening night audience. The crimson draperies that had preceded them were shipped to Atlanta, where the company has played for twenty-nine seasons.

The following year the first rows of the orchestra seats were removed to make room for the increased orchestra called for by *Salome*.

Herbert Witherspoon,
distinguished basso,
executive for a few weeks.

Giulio Gatti-Casazza, as he looked
in 1908, imperturbable, enigmatic.

Edward Johnson greeted his difficult
duties in 1935 with a gay smile.

When the newly formed Metropolitan Opera Company took over the Conried organization in 1908, it invited the new impresario, Giulio Gatti-Casazza, to visit the scene of his future labors. The reticent manager praised the auditorium. "It is indeed a noble house," he exclaimed. Yet his trained eye saw the need for many improvements, which were speedily installed.

An unfailing ally stood behind the General Manager in the person of Otto H. Kahn, the newly elected President of the Board, who had served as a director of the producing company since 1903 and who now initiated nearly a quarter of a century of service as its dominant figure.

In the season of 1908-09 family circle subscribers were enabled for the first time to reach their exalted seats by means of two large electric elevators. Many of those who sat in the new folding orchestra chairs enjoyed better visibility through the rearrangement of their seats. The new conductor, Arturo Toscanini, could profit by the new mechanism which raised and lowered the orchestra pit in accordance with the requirements of the score. One and all could admire the ceiling and walls of the auditorium, redecorated by Carrère and Hastings.

The following September a less obvious improvement added to the smoothness of production. A commodious rehearsal room was built on the corner of Fortieth Street and Seventh Avenue. This proved so useful that a similar "roof stage" was constructed by the firm of Perry Reid on the southwest corner of the theatre in 1921, with a metal bridge connecting the two above the stage.

The fact that no other major structural changes in the Opera House were made for the next ten years is in part explained by Mr. Kahn's prevailing interest in a possible new opera house, an ambition which was not to be gratified because of the economic problems involved.

Indeed by the time of his resignation in 1932, the effects of the depression menaced the very continuance of opera. Soon after the formation of the Metropolitan Opera Association under the chairmanship of Mr. Kahn's successor, Paul D. Cravath, the new helmsman notified R. Fulton Cutting, chairman of the real estate company which owned the house, that opera at the Metropolitan would have to be abandoned. Cornelius N. Bliss, Jr., a box-holder and member of the real estate board, proposed the organization of a joint committee of the real estate company and the Opera Association to study the situation and recommend a plan to avert the catastrophe. Mr. Cutting persuaded Mr. Bliss to serve as chairman of this committee. A campaign organization was set up with Miss Lucrezia Bori as chairman. In 1933 a fund of $300,000 was raised by public subscription to keep opera alive through the depression. Meanwhile Mr. Bliss was elected Chairman of the Executive Committee and finally persuaded to become Chairman of the Board by Mr. Cravath, who himself became president.

In Mr. Gatti's final season, 1934-35, important improvements were carried out under the supervision of the J. G. White Construction Company, A new asbestos curtain was hung, terrazzo flooring was provided for the outer lobbies; the north, south and east fronts of the building were cleaned by sandblasting; new sponsor could be found for the Saturday broadcasts. He also led a brilliant campaign over the air in support of the plan to purchase the theatre, which resulted in a third of the total proceeds, while an equal amount was credited to The Metropolitan Opera Guild. Half of the amount raised went into down payments on the house itself, which was purchased by the Metropolitan Opera Association from the Metropolitan Opera and Real Estate Company. For the first time since the fire of 1892, the organization which owned the house was also responsible for the production of opera.

The major changes in the construction of the theatre which were made possible by the 1940 campaign have proved a wise investment of the $130,000 allotted to them. The grand tier boxes, whose popular appeal had dwindled, were abolished, and 144 stationary seats were installed to replace them, centered about a convenient broadcasting box, arranged by the National Broadcasting Company and strategically placed for ultimate television use. Opposite the omnibus box used by the Metropolitan Opera Club, four rows of 56 seats were placed at the disposal of The Metropolitan Opera Guild in a single unit, to be known as the Guild Box. Across the grand tier foyer the Metropolitan Opera Guild clubroom was constructed and attractively decorated. New maroon carpeting and cheerful cream paint brightened all the corridors while the columns and rails were neatly recovered. Outside the building the porte-cocheres were reconstructed. For the first time, the box office was given improved ventilation and indirect lighting.

One of the most interesting improvements of the 1940-41 season was the set of new gold damask curtains, an exact reproduction of those which had hung across the stage since 1905. Once more The Metropolitan Opera Guild stepped into the picture and asked for the shabby remnants of the old fabric. The material was cut into practicable sizes, cleaned and sold in small samples to opera-lovers all over the world. More than $8000 has been raised through this project and expended both for opera tickets for music students and additional stage training for young members of the company.

The withdrawal of the Metropolitan Opera and Real Estate Company following the sale of the opera house, where it had occupied offices at the northwest corner of the building, permitted this part of the structure to be rented.

In 1942 the trust company which had occupied the southeast corner of the opera house for many years, terminated its lease. In the autumn of 1943 a textile firm rented the property and installed streamlined display windows.

Thus with constantly freshened demeanor, and gradually expanding capacity the Metropolitan Opera House stands in its maturity. Built in the eighties at the northwestern extremity of social New York it has watched the residential center of the city pass far northward. Two railway terminals remain in its neighborhood, two subways flank its walls, bus lines serve it on three sides. The nobility of a bygone age, with its tiaras and tailcoats, has passed away, but new crowds surge through its doorways to gain blessings from what is still "a noble house."

seats were placed in the orchestra; a circulating ice-water system was installed; a fresh coat of gray-green paint was applied to the lobbies. Even more radical was the modernization of the electric equipment on the stage.

The following year, under Edward Johnson, who took over the management after the brief administration and untimely death of Herbert Witherspoon, the construction program was completed, while the newly formed Metropolitan Opera Guild contributed a cyclorama to add effectiveness to the stage picture. A new ventilating system utilized a special device for washing air by steam. A series of Micromax gauges enabled the engineer to regulate the temperature and humidity in all parts of the house. The roofs were covered with rubberoid and slate. Padded chairs were placed for the first time in the family circle.

In 1937 the Opera Guild provided the means to modernize the room used by the orchestra below the stage. The buffet lounge was also decorated.

In 1940 a nation-wide campaign for funds to purchase the building from the real estate company resulted in gifts of $1,057,000 from 166,000 donors. George A. Sloan successfully presided as chairman of the drive and in September was elected President of the Association to succeed Mr. Cravath. Another member of the Board of Directors, David Sarnoff, made a most important contribution. The National Broadcasting Company, of which he was president, presented Metropolitan Opera as a sustaining program during the difficult days when no

New light was shed on the old Opera House in 1949, when a skyscraper was in progress.

The Curtain Rises

METROPOLITAN OPERA has come to stand for six outstanding characteristics: a balanced international repertory, offered in the original language and brightened by musical novelties, the distinction of leading European artists, the recognition of fresh young talent and Americans on the roster.

On October 22, 1883, when General Manager Henry E. Abbey watched the curtain rise on his initial presentation of *Faust*, he could have congratulated himself that he was about to establish a precedent for four of these traditions, although two of them were as yet in embryo.

It is true that his organization was known as "Abbey's Italian Opera Company." It is true that all of the nineteen operas which he presented in the fourteen weeks of his winter and spring seasons in New York were given in Italian. But his repertory did include seven French works and even a single German music drama, *Lohengrin*, which shared first honors with *Faust* in warranting no less than six performances.

The single musical novelty, Ponchielli's *La Gioconda*, according to Henry E. Krehbiel, the chief historian of the period, "was performed (on December 20) with a gorgeousness of stage appointments and a strength of ensemble which spoke volumes for the earnestness of the effort which Mr. Abbey was making to give grand opera in a style worthy of the American metropolis." The public response was indicated by a capacity house.

The cast included several of the artists who had appeared in the opening night *Faust*. Christine Nilsson, a great lady of the contemporary stage, had been thirteen years before the American public, but "her art had grown in dignity and nobility with the years." Sofia Scalchi, whose graceful Siébel had long been a favorite, was La Cieca. Giuseppe Del Puente and Franco Novara again made a favorable impression in their baritone and bass roles.

Mr. Abbey also boasted in his ranks the presence of a renowned Italian tenor, Italo Campanini, his first Faust and Lohengrin, the older brother of Cleofonte Campanini, who occasionally replaced Auguste Vianesi at the podium. Another stellar tenor was the Frenchman Victor Capoul, the first Metropolitan Wilhelm Meister and "the most fascinating lover known to opera in America."

Emmy Fursch-Madi, the first Donna Anna of the house, was characterized as "one of the finest singers in her style and one of the most conscientious artists known to her period." Zelia Trebelli, the dramatic mezzo who created Carmen at the Metropolitan, had earned sufficient fame to have the composer Thomas write the Rondo Gavotte in *Mignon* especially for her.

Of the younger singers, the most outstanding was, of course, Marcella Sembrich, not yet twenty-six years of age, but with six years of leading operatic roles behind her in such cities as Athens, Dresden and London. In that inaugural Metropolitan season Mme. Sembrich lent her "exquisite style," "velvety" yet "brilliant" voice and "thoroughly musical nature" to ten roles, Lucia, Rosina, Zerlina, Margherita di Valois, as the florid queen of *Les Huguenots* was called, Martha, Gilda, la Sonnambula, Violetta and a single Elvira in *I Puritani* and Ophelia in *Hamlet*. Such was the remarkable introduction of an artist who was to return modestly to further study in Milan, win new glories in the European capitals and come back to the Metropolitan stage fifteen years later for a full decade of superb performances.

The story of Mme. Sembrich's astonishing versatility in a concert arranged as a benefit for Mr. Abbey on April 21, 1884, to help make up the manager's deficit

Italo Campanini, seen here as Don José, still showed something of his "old-time sweetness" and "manly ring" in the opening night Faust.

"There is no resisting" Christine Nilsson as "Goethe's sweet child," wrote Krehbiel after the inaugural performance of Faust.

Marcella Sembrich, the Metropolitan's first Lucia, is shown here as Ulana, heroine of Paderewski's opera Manru, *introduced in 1902.*

for the season, cannot be told too often. Having sung the Lesson Scene from *The Barber*, she played a violin obbligato to Mme. Nilsson's performance of the Bach-Gounod *Ave Maria* and reappeared to toss off a Chopin Mazurka at the piano.

To conclude the list of Metropolitan traditions which became evident in the first season of the theatre was the presence of at least one American in the company. This was Alwina Valleria, born Miss Schoening of Baltimore, who had made her American debut at the Academy of Music four years earlier, after considerable European success. She was the first Metropolitan Leonora in *Trovatore*, Philine and Micaela, a role which she had balked at singing in London with Minnie Hauk, suggesting that it be given instead to a chorister!

It has been stated that Henry Abbey lost $600,000 in his first Metropolitan season, due partly to the large fees which he paid his artists (over $1000 a performance to Nilsson and Campanini), partly to his elaborate settings and costumes (Lilli Lehmann stated that every dress came from Worth in Paris) and possibly also to the deficits of his sixty-nine performances in eight cities on tour.

To his credit must be cited what Mr. Krehbiel has called "his heroic effort to galvanize Italian opera, which seemed moribund, into vitality. . . . His stage sets were uniformly handsome; . . . his orchestra, though faulty in composition as well as execution, did some admirable work; . . . his chorus was prompt, vigorous and tuneful; his ensembles were carefully and intelligently composed, and his selection of operas was judicious. . . . He gave to New York the strongest combination of woman singers that the city had ever known."

The Metropolitan tradition was established.

Gold From The Rhine

DISCIPLINE UNDER LEOPOLD DAMROSCH, 1884-85

THE SECOND ERA of Metropolitan Opera history opened with an economic compromise: it generated one of the richest artistic contributions in the life of the opera house.

After the financial fiasco of Henry Abbey, the Metropolitan directors turned to Ernest Gye of London to steer their second season. They did not learn of his refusal till the summer of 1884. The situation grew tense. At length Leopold Damrosch, the revered conductor of the New York Symphony Orchestra, suggested that he might assemble a company of German singers, competent to present the German music dramas. The directors were tempted by the inexpensiveness of the project. At three days' notice Dr. Damrosch set out for Europe and returned with the contracts of Amalia Materna, the original Bayreuth Kundry; Marianne Brandt, her successor in the role and a fine contralto; Auguste Kraus, the young wife of the conductor Anton Seidl, soon to be the first Sieglinde of the Metropolitan; Anton Schott, its first Siegmund; Josef Staudigl, its first Wotan and among others Marie Schröder-Hanfstängl, a second dramatic soprano to sing in *Les Huguenots*, *La Juive* and Donna Anna in *Don Giovanni*.

Dr. Damrosch opened his season on November 17 by conducting *Tannhäuser*, which to all but the Germans present "was practically a novelty." Two days later he followed it by a *Fidelio* with Mme. Brandt and later *Der Freischütz*, *Lohengrin* and *Die Walküre*, varying the German fare with seven operas from the Italian and French repertories, all however, sung in German.

The German language was not the only innovation of the season. In the words of Walter Damrosch, who helped his father as assistant conductor and chorus master, the chief contribution of the year was the introduction of "a new standard of balanced production with little emphasis on the stars and a great deal of disciplined rehearsal. Our singers were very amenable to ensemble work, carrying out the dramatic side of their work with real ability."

As the final *Tannhäuser* of the subscription season was being set up on the stage on February 11, Dr. Damrosch, exhausted by overwork, contracted pneumonia and died four days later. His baton was taken over that night by his twenty-three year old son, who subsequently conducted the performances which the company played on tour.

Auguste Seidl-Kraus, a plump Eva, with Emil Fischer, first Hans Sachs at the Metropolitan.

"Her voice glorified the music," wrote the Tribune critic of Lilli Lehmann's Brünnhilde.

ANTON SEIDL INTRODUCES *Die Meistersinger* 1885-86

Encouraged by the small deficit and the high artistic achievement of their first German season, the Metropolitan directors appointed their secretary, Edmund C. Stanton, as salaried director and suggested that he and young Walter Damrosch go abroad to seek additional talent.

In a few weeks Damrosch obtained commitments from Anton Seidl, a former secretary of Richard Wagner and now foremost champion of his music dramas; Max Alvary, later to prove himself an ideal Siegfried; Emil Fischer, the first American Hans Sachs; and the heroic soprano, Lilli Lehmann.

The season which followed is remembered today for its introduction of *Die Meistersinger* on January 4, 1886. In spite of the strangeness of its idiom and the epical demands it made on the concentration of the public, the work achieved eight performances. Even more popular proved another novelty of the season, Goldmark's *Queen of Sheba*, whose magnificent production (said to have cost

$75,000), was witnessed fifteen times and presented in Chicago and St. Louis.

An unusual variation on the German works was a German version of *Carmen,* in which Lehmann chose to make her debut on November 25, and also a German *Faust* on January 20, when the majestic soprano sang Marguerite in an uncut edition of the seven-act work.

To Walter Damrosch it was given to conduct the first Metropolitan *Parsifal,* presented in concert form, with the Oratorio Society singing the choruses in English and the Metropolitan artists filling the principal roles in German.

NIEMANN AND LEHMANN, THE FIRST AMERICAN TRISTAN AND ISOLDE 1886-87

The third German season was momentous for the arrival of the heroic tenor, Albert Niemann, who at the age of fifty-seven still added the enthusiasm of a youth to the skill and sincerity of a great singing actor. After a brilliant Metropolitan debut as Siegmund on November 10, he rose to new heights in what Edgar Stillman Kelley described as "the most important event in the history of the lyric stage in America." This was the first *Tristan und Isolde* on December 1, with Lehmann, Brandt, Fischer and Robinson singing with Niemann under Seidl's baton. Another newcomer of the season was Mme. Herbert-Förster, whose husband Victor Herbert then served as first cellist in the orchestra.

An operatic novelty of the year eventually outran *Tristan* in popularity and has steadily held first place in the entire list of Metropolitan favorites. This was, of course, *Aïda,* which was introduced by Seidl on November 12 in German.

One hundred and thirty-seven thousand, three hundred and ninety-nine opera-lovers who purchased tickets that year at prices ranging from 50¢ to $4.00 might have read a prophecy of the ultimate return of Italian opera and the stellar presence of Adelina Patti in a special season successfully presented by Henry Abbey in April at a $7.00 top. They had been reassured, however, by the Metropolitan directorate that opera would be continued in German for three years.

Siegfried AND *Götterdämmerung* 1887-88

Although the music dramas of Richard Wagner continued to nourish the Metropolitan public as staple fare, it was now decided to lighten the repertory with such works as Halévy's *La Juive,* Nessler's *The Trumpeter of Sackingen,* Spontini's *Ferdinando Cortez* and Weber's *Euryanthe.*

Far more significant was Seidl's introduction of *Siegfried* on November 9 and *Götterdämmerung* on January 25 with Lilli Lehmann singing both the Brünnhildes, Max Alvary the younger and Niemann the elder Siegfried. In *Götterdämmerung* both the Norn and Waltraute scenes were omitted, for it seemed better, as Mr. Krehbiel remarked, "to achieve success for the representations by adapting the drama to the capacity of the public than to sacrifice it bodily on the altar of integrity!"

THE FIRST *Ring* CYCLE 1888-89

A sixteen-week season, the longest that the Metropolitan Opera House had thus far known, indicated the growing public response to Wagner's "music of the future" as interpreted by Anton Seidl and his artists.

The introduction of *Das Rheingold* on January 4 provoked a series of contrasting adjectives from the press. Some reviewers called it "a failure," "barren," "abstruse"; others described it as "a grand spectacular exhibition and no less an event of the highest artistic importance."

Rheingold also served to usher in a precedent which has become an integral part of Metropolitan tradition, the performance of the entire *Ring of the Nibelung* cycle. The *Ring* was twice presented in the spring of 1889, with the season extended an additional week to make the repetition possible.

THE ITALIAN TIDE GATHERS STRENGTH 1889-90

The ten Wagner music dramas from *Rienzi* to *Götterdämmerung* still held first places in public favor and were presented by Mr. Seidl this season.

In *The Flying Dutchman* a new baritone, Theodor Reichmann, made his debut in the title role on opening night, November 27. This occasion also served to inaugurate another innovation. For the first time since the opening season, the pit was lowered, never again to obstruct the view of the stage.

One novelty of the season, Cornelius' charming *Barber of Bagdad*, was performed January 3, conducted by Mr. Damrosch. Another, Verdi's *Masked Ball*, started its long if intermittent career at the Opera House on December 11 as *Der Maskenball*, while a third, Bellini's *Norma*, was offered on February 27 as a nonsubscription benefit for Lilli Lehmann who sang the title role.

Another spring season of Italian opera, centering about Mme. Patti, was presented this year by Henry Abbey, who now added the name of his associate Maurice Grau to his letterhead. The twenty-one performances started on March 24 with the first Metropolitan *Otello*, featuring the powerful Francesco Tamagno in the title role and Emma Albani as Desdemona. Another outstanding event was the *Trovatore* in which Lillian Nordica made her debut at the Opera House.

THE PUBLIC STRIKES FOR WAGNER 1890-91

Two opposing forces were evolving in the Metropolitan audience, with the bewildered manager, Edmund Stanton, endeavoring to pacify them both. In the boxes sat the stockholders, bored by the length of the Wagnerian music dramas, hungry for novelty and entertainment, and anxious to chat between arias.

To please them Mr. Stanton brought over from Europe three little known operas. One was Franchetti's *Asrael,* in which the versatile tenor Andreas Dippel made his debut on the opening night, November 27, initiating a career which covered eighteen seasons and culminated with his sharing managerial duties with Guilio Gatti-Casazza in 1908. Even shorter lived than *Asrael* were Smareglia's *Vassall von Szigeth* and the Duke of Saxe-Coburg's *Diana von Solange*.

Stanton also determined to lay aside the heavier Wagnerian dramas, postponing *Die Meistersinger* until mid-January. Soon came the announcement that

Minnie Hauk gave Carmen "an impersonation of marked and fascinating individuality," wrote Mr. Krehbiel in the Tribune, *noting that her "freakishness of tempo" was justified.*

opera in German would be replaced the next season by Italian and French works.

Confronted with this prospect, the public rose in its wrath, crowded every Wagnerian performance, cheered Mr. Seidl each time he conducted and flocked three hundred strong to sign a petition to have the next *Diana* replaced by *Fidelio*.

One great artist proved acceptable to both groups. This was the renowned Minnie Hauk, the most famous Carmen before Calvé, who joined what she described as "the Herrs, Fraus and Fräuleins" of the Company to sing *l'Africana* and *Carmen*, her final operatic appearances in her native New York.

With a last tumultuous *Meistersinger* on March 21, the seven years of opera in German at the Metropolitan came to a close. The German plan had not proved self-sustaining, nor was it sufficiently attractive to the stockholders to warrant their continued subsidy. The receipts of the Wagnerian performances had grown from year to year, but the total receipts had waned.

On the other side of the record stood a magnificent monument to artistic integrity, an edifice founded by Leopold Damrosch, reared by Anton Seidl and embellished by some of the greatest interpreters in Wagnerian history.

But the ideal balance of an international company had not yet been struck.

24

Fabulous Starlight

SINCE HIS ORIGINAL disastrous Metropolitan season, Henry E. Abbey had been encouraged in the production of opera by the success of his two tentative visits to the opera house in 1887 and 1890. He had also found strength in the support of his associate Maurice Grau, who with John B. Schoeffel of Boston as silent partner, now found a place of leadership in the Metropolitan management.

After five performances in Milwaukee, following the thirteen in Chicago, the three partners opened their thirteen-week season in New York. The opening night *Roméo* on December 14 disclosed three of their brightest stars — twenty-four-year-old Emma Eames, cool and beautiful, fresh from her Paris triumphs under the coaching of Gounod himself; Jean de Reszke, the romantic ideal of all Roméos; and his brother, the magnificent bass, Edouard. This same matchless trio was united in its first *Faust* on February 1.

From the German company remained Lilli Lehmann and her husband, the tenor Paul Kalisch, to present *Fidelio, Norma, Don Giovanni* and *Trovatore* in Italian. Another survivor was Anton Seidl, who was now called on to conduct *Die Meistersinger* under the name *I Maestri Cantori*.

It was now that the brilliant dramatic soprano Lillian Nordica made her official debut as a member of the company in *Les Huguenots* on December 18, while Emma Albani also reappeared, as a Metropolitan star, in the role of Marguerite on January 6. A third American prima donna was the diminutive coloratura Marie Van Zandt, who sang La Sonnambula and Lakmé, the role which Delibes had written for her and which she had created in Paris.

Another powerful attraction in the roster was Jean Lassalle, the heroic French baritone who made his debut as Nelusko with Nordica and both de Reszkes in the memorable *l'Africana* on January 15.

The two novelties of the season were a rather casual *Orfeo* and a *Cavalleria* which had not yet found its perfect cast.

The Metropolitan Opera House was dark during the season 1892-93 because of the reorganization and reconstruction made necessary by the fire.

On November 27, 1893, the theatre reopened under the management of Abbey, Schoeffel and Grau with a *Faust* even more brilliant than that of the inaugural season. Here were Eames and the de Reszkes, Lassalle as Valentin, the handsome Olympia Guercia making her debut as Siébel with the versatile Bauermeister as Marta, singing under a new and eloquent conductor, Luigi Mancinelli, who shared the Italian repertory with Emilio Bevignani.

Two days later a bevy of new stars appeared in the operatic heavens. An incandescent influence on Metropolitan history glowed in the person of Emma Calvé, who sang her first Santuzza on November 29 and less than a month later her first Carmen. The dynamic temperament and colorful yet disciplined art of this Frenchwoman largely accounts for the popularity of the Bizet drama, which was played thirty-eight times during the next four years, leading even *Faust* in public demand.

Almost equally magnetic was the phenomenal basso, Pol Plançon, who combined the power of the dramatic voice with the elegance of a lyricist and the perfect articulation and projection of a coloratura. It has been said that "no prima donna could equal his trill." Best of his thirty-one roles was Méphistophélès. Of briefer stay was the mellow lyric soprano, Sigrid Arnoldson. A majestic luminary was the Australian soprano, Nellie Melba, who was hailed as the "finest exponent of vocalization since Sembrich" when she made her debut as Lucia on December 4, opening a Metropolitan career which lasted until 1910.

At the close of the season Walter Damrosch returned with some of the earlier Wagnerian troupe to present *Götterdämmerung* on March 28. The following month, after the regular company had returned from a tour of fifty performances in Boston, Chicago and St. Louis, it played a supplementary season, offering the first American performance of *Werther* on April 19 with Eames, Arnoldson and Jean de Reszke.

The brilliance of these great names must not blind us to the other contributions which the Metropolitan was making to opera. The claim to a cosmopolitan repertory was upheld by six French and three German works as well as the ten Italian operas while the influx of French artists meant that at least some of the principals in such a work as *Carmen* might be heard in its original language.

The season 1894-95 was made especially illustrious by the addition to the company of two distinguished baritones. One was the consummate artist Victor Maurel, who made his debut on December 3 as Iago, opposite the Otello of Francesco Tamagno, now for the first time a regular member of the company, and Emma Eames as Desdemona. Mr. Maurel was also featured in the chief artistic event of the season, the North American premiere of Verdi's *Falstaff* on February 4, in which the other newcomer, the lyric baritone Giuseppe Campanari, sang the role of Ford. A third news event was the introduction of Saint-Saëns' *Samson et Dalila* in operatic form on February 8.

During the company's extended spring tour Walter Damrosch leased the Metropolitan Opera House for a successful Wagner season, interesting for the

Edouard de Reszke made Méphistophélès a cynical but polished gentleman with an evil laugh.

Lillian Nordica, "lily of the north," as they called her in Italy, in the role of Selika.

Emma Eames was proud of her Aïda make-up, which did not mar her beauty as the Ethiopian slave.

Jean de Reszke's Roméo brought palpitations of joy to every lady in the house—and critics too.

debut of Johanna Gadski. After this the regular company returned for an additional fortnight.

The stimulating effect of Mr. Damrosch's month of Wagner may be guessed from the Metropolitan prospectus for 1895-96, which announced that new German artists and a German chorus would make German opera possible in the original language.

Tristan und Isolde opened the season on November 27 under Seidl's baton with Jean and Edouard de Reszke singing in German for the first time and Lillian Nordica as the Isolde, indicating that the new German artists were less vital to the project than the great international artists already in the company. The same trio was also responsible for the *Lohengrin* which followed and also for the same stellar *Huguenots* which Mancinelli had introduced the preceding year with Melba, Scalchi, Plançon and Maurel — truly a "night of the seven stars."

The final season of the Abbey, Schoeffel and Grau management, 1896-97, was darkened by a series of disasters. First came the death of the soprano Katerina Klafsky, an importation of Mr. Damrosch who was to have sung Wagnerian roles opposite Jean de Reszke. Next followed the death of Henry Abbey himself, soon followed by William Steinway, who had been of great assistance in the management's financial affairs. Then Lillian Nordica withdrew, discomfited by the rumor that Mme. Melba had been given the exclusive rights to the *Siegfried* Brünnhilde. When Melba sang the role on December 30, she promptly collapsed from its exhausting demands on her light coloratura voice and a fortnight later retired for the rest of the season. Emma Eames then fell ill and a

An unusual picture of Nellie Melba as Rosina, a role which she never sang at the Metropolitan.

Emma Calvé's Carmen "is a creature of unbridled passion . . . careless of all consequences." Times.

projected *Nozze di Figaro* was withdrawn. During the performance of *Marta* which was substituted for it, the French baritone Armand Castelmary fell on the stage with a heart attack and died in the arms of Jean de Reszke. The four-week Chicago visit proved so ruinous that the de Reszkes and others subscribed $30,000 to pull the management through.

In spite of these calamities, the Metropolitan season was sustained for its thirteen weeks and even brightened by a novelty. On February 12 Massenet's *Le Cid* was introduced with the de Reszkes and Pol Plançon singing their original roles. Lassalle was the King and two fine sopranos, the lusty Slavic Felia Litvinne and the flute-like Clementine deVere took the women's parts.

THE FIRMAMENT OF MAURICE GRAU 1898-1903

No Metropolitan opera company played in the opera house during the season of 1897-98, although the theatre was leased to an organization formed by Walter Damrosch and Charles A. Ellis.

The cause of Wagner music dramas experienced a severe loss on March 28 in the sudden death of Anton Seidl whose funeral services at the Metropolitan were as impressive as those of Leopold Damrosch, thirteen years before.

The following month the directors of the Metropolitan Opera and Real Estate Company approved a lease of the auditorium to Maurice Grau for three years. Neither death, financial disaster nor delay could further postpone the golden era.

With unerring judgment Mr. Grau recalled the most popular and useful artists of earlier season: Marcella Sembrich, Lilli Lehmann and the reliable Andreas Dippel. From the former administration he retained Nordica, Eames, Plançon, the de Reszkes and Campanari. From the Damrosch-Ellis Company he secured the authoritative baritone, David Bispham.

He also introduced several distinguished newcomers: Ernestine Schumann-Heink, the powerful yet velvet-voiced contralto; Anton van Rooy, a dark-voiced Dutch Wotan; the dramatic French tenor Albert Saléza; Ernst Van Dyck, the opening night Tannhäuser; and Suzanne Adams, a young soprano from Cambridge, Mass., whose "grace and purity of phrasing" were evidenced from her first Juliette with the de Reszkes. To replace Mr. Seidl at the podium, Grau engaged the renowned Viennese conductor, Franz Schalk.

The season's single novelty, *Ero e Leandro,* conducted by its composer, Luigi Mancinelli, was less significant, in spite of its libretto by Boito, than the extraordinary casts with which the classic operas were presented: *Tannhäuser,* with Eames, Nordica, Van Dyck and Plançon; *The Barber* with Sembrich, Thomas Salignac, Campanari and Edouard de Reszke; *Die Walküre* with Eames, Lehmann, Van Dyck and Van Rooy; *Tristan* with Nordica or Lehmann, the de Reszkes and Bispham or Van Rooy; *Don Giovanni* with Lehmann, Sembrich, Nordica, Maurel, Salignac and Edouard de Reszke.

To the present generation these Olympian casts may seem as dim as Biblical genealogies or the roster of Homeric heroes. To the recording collector they recall the tones of flutes and trumpets, highly polished voices, emitted with the florid accuracy of a coloratura, slightly covered, remote, perhaps a trifle cold. To our parents and grandparents they suggested a great hierarchy of full bosomed prima donnas and bearded princes: ladies who were "respectfully invited to sing," gentlemen who wore silk hats at rehearsal; divas and *primi tenori assoluti* who stood squarely facing the audience, bestowing their high C's without fear or favor. Theirs was the grandeur of grand opera.

In Maurice Grau's second season, 1899-1900, the rich resources of his company permitted him to give the three major Mozart operas. First of these was *Don Giovanni,* with the dramatic baritone Antonio Scotti making his debut in the title role on December 27 and thus starting one of the longest and most honorable of operatic careers — nearly thirty-three years at the Metropolitan. *Le Nozze di Figaro* followed on December 22 with Eames, de Lussan, de Vere-Sapio, Campanari and Edouard de Reszke. *The Magic Flute* was introduced for the first time on the 30th of March, with no less than five American women in the cast: Emma Eames as Pamina, the sprightly New Yorker Zélie de Lussan as Papagena, the contraltos Carrie Bridewell from Mississippi and Eleanore Broadfoot from New York with Suzanne Adams in important ensemble roles.

Another Metropolitan novelty, Nicolai's *Merry Wives of Windsor,* did not endure beyond its premiere on March 9.

In the absence of Jean de Reszke from the company a new French tenor, Albert Alvarez, undertook the leading lyric roles.

The Wagnerian repertory was delayed by the illness of Milka Ternina, the sensitive Croatian soprano, who could not make her debut until a *Tannhäuser* on January 27, but later sang with great success in both *Ring* Cycles led by Emil Paur. Three Evas lent variety to the season's *Meistersinger*: in January Emma Eames, in February Johanna Gadski, who had made her official Metropolitan debut as Senta in *The Flying Dutchman* on January 6, and in March Marcella Sembrich, who thus offered her one Wagnerian role in the opera house.

In spite of the longest tour yet made by a Metropolitan company — seventy-seven performances in eighteen cities before the New York season, twenty-one performances in Philadelphia during the winter and ten more in three cities in April — the New York season was this year extended to fifteen weeks.

The season of 1900-01 was also prefaced by a tour, this time made up of forty-one performances in six cities, including twenty-four in San Francisco.

The list of distinguished newcomers was lengthened still further. In the opening night *Roméo* on December 18, Mr. Grau presented a new light baritone, the razor-tongued, giant-voiced Charles Gilibert. Four days later he introduced a young contralto from Pittsburgh, fresh from European apprenticeship, Louise Homer, whose Amneris initiated a career which endured for nearly thirty years. At that same *Aïda* appeared a new bass baritone, the richly endowed yet highly conscientious Marcel Journet. Within the week the captivating soubrette Fritzi Scheff opened the first of her three Metropolitan seasons as Marzellina in *Fidelio.*

Of great significance in the future development of the Metropolitan repertory was the introduction of the Puccini operas this season with *La Bohème,* presented on December 26 with Melba, Saléza and Campanari, and *Tosca* which received its North American premiere on February 4 with Milka Ternina and Antonio Scotti.

The return of Jean de Reszke for his final American season drew capacity audiences to half a dozen different Wagnerian dramas, conducted by Walter Damrosch as well as to *Faust, Aïda, Roméo* and *Les Huguenots.* The great tenor was joined by his brother in their first German *Meistersinger* on March 25, as well as in Jean's last *Lohengrin* on March 29.

A gala performance of acts from different operas, presented in honor of Prince Henry of Prussia, brother of the German Emperor, on February 25, 1902, seems to have eclipsed the operatic news events of the following season.

Historically the year was noteworthy for the introduction of Paderewski's opera *Manru* and de Lara's *Messalina.* Musically, it is remembered rather for the first Metropolitan production of Donizetti's *La Fille du Régiment,* in which Mme. Sembrich found one of her happiest roles.

Maurice Grau's final season, 1902-03, was the longest which the Opera House had thus far known: ninety-five performances of thirty-two operas in seventeen weeks. The annual tour was accordingly reduced to thirty-seven performances in March and April, with twenty representations given in Philadelphia.

Plans for cycles of Mozart and Verdi had to be modified, but seven operas by the Italian composer were presented, including the Metropolitan's first *Ernani* on January 28 and first Italian *Ballo in Maschera* on February 23.

Of profound importance in the history of the house was the appearance of a new Wagner conductor, the stocky, bearded Alfred Hertz. With *Lohengrin,* on November 28, he started a Metropolitan career which endured fourteen years.

Of the three tenors who were introduced to fill Jean de Reszke's roles, the most valuable proved to be Alois Burgstaller. The first newcomer, Georg Anthes, is especially remembered for his misfortune with the *Siegfried* anvil, which refused to break at the blow of the sword.

Sembrich's first Mimi and Eames' first Tosca were among the most prized feminine contributions, while the repertory momentarily included the only opera presented at the Metropolitan by a woman composer, Ethel Smyth's *Der Wald.*

Meanwhile Mr. Grau's health was rapidly failing under the strain of his operatic duties. In April the company gathered to present him with a farewell gala performance. Then he retired to his home near Paris where he died in 1907.

Maurice Grau has gone into history as a collector of stars, a shrewd business man and skillful diplomat in dealing with temperaments. It must be admitted that his novelties were few and the development of his orchestra and ensemble incidental. The variety of talent at his disposal enabled him to present Wagner in German, *Carmen* and *Roméo* in French. He introduced Puccini to Metropolitan audiences, stressed Mozart and Verdi, offered the first unabridged *Ring*

Ernestine Schumann-Heink and Johanna Gadski sang their first Metropolitan Meistersinger *together in 1900 under Emil Paur.*

Antonio Scotti was hailed at his debut as Don Giovanni in 1899 for "courtly ease."

Milka Ternina sang only four seasons at the Opera House. Her Brünnhilde was tender, tragic.

of the Nibelung. He took his company from coast to coast. In the starlight which flooded his stage we must not lose sight of the high artistic achievement and broad vision of the man who had made it possible.

HEINRICH CONRIED DEALS IN *Parsifal* AND PERSONALITIES 1903-08

The first of three important innovations in the initial season of Heinrich Conried's Metropolitan Opera management did not at once suggest the importance it was later to assume. This was the organization of a producing company whose title for the first time included the word "Metropolitan." This corporation leased the theatre from the Metropolitan Opera and Real Estate Company as the previous managers had done, but although it was first known as the Conried Metropolitan Company, it proved independent of any specific impresario, and thus established a basic continuity in the administration of the Opera House.

The second was the engagement of Enrico Caruso, who brought his matchless voice to the Metropolitan and sang with ever increasing artistry for nearly twenty years. It was actually Maurice Grau who had first offered Caruso a contract for forty performances at approximately $960 a performance, and the frugal Conried who succeeded in reducing this ambitious assignment to twenty-five.

At the opening night *Rigoletto* on November 23, 1903, the gifted Neapolitan was hailed as a "manly singer, with a voice of fine quality". . ."capable of intelligence and passion". . . with "clear and pealing high tones."

The third innovation of Conried's first year was the American stage premiere of *Parsifal*. This was offered on Christmas Eve, after elaborate preparations. The performance was greeted with reverence, the *Times* affirming the "universally compelling potency of the score" and the production winning unstinted praise.

The original cast, which was most often heard at the repetitions that followed, was headed by Alois Burgstaller and Milka Ternina, while Otto Goritz made his debut as the first American Klingsor.

Conried's new German conductor Felix Mottl — also listed in the prospectus as general music director — helped Alfred Hertz prepare the work, lending his score for the purpose, with Wagner's personal directions in his own hand. Hertz was accorded "most lavish praise" by the press and entrusted with all the fifty-two *Parsifals* of his thirteen years at the Metropolitan — no small compensation for his debarrment from Germany as the conductor of the forbidden work.

Another great addition to the Wagnerian wing was Olive Fremstad, the dramatic Swedish soprano, who did not sing Kundry until the following season, but won instantaneous recognition for the tender Sieglinde of her debut under Mottl in the November 25 *Walküre* as well as her passionate Venus and Santuzza. Calvé's return accounted for the reappearance of her unforgettable *Carmen*, while Sembrich and Scotti embellished many of the performances which Arturo Vigna conducted for Caruso.

Caruso's unfaltering appeal for the public is indicated by the increased number of performances for which he was engaged in Conried's second season, 1904-05, which opened with a triumphant *Aïda* on November 21, when the tenor sang with Eames, Scotti and Plançon. It is also suggested by the increase of his remuneration, now set at $1152 a performance and rising ten years later to $2500.

A series of misadventures occasioned an extraordinary record this year for Andreas Dippel, who was often called on to replace other tenors and thus sang sixteen different leading roles in three languages during the year.

On the bright side of the ledger was the continued presence of so many notable artists in the company that Conried not only staged a *Huguenots* on February 3 with Sembrich, Nordica, Caruso, Plançon, Journet, Edyth Walker and Scotti, but actually displayed his stars as supers in a gala performance of *Die Fledermaus*.

Lighter operas found their way to the repertory during the season of 1905-06 as vehicles for Caruso, whose forty appearances attracted capacity houses, no matter what work was announced. *La Favorita, La Sonnambula* and *Marta* were restored during the winter especially for the star.

A sturdier precedent in the musical life of the theatre was set by *Hänsel und Gretel* which was introduced on November 25, in the presence of the composer, Engelbert Humperdinck.

Five New Yorkers were meanwhile filling important places in the company. Bessie Abott, a lyric soprano from Riverside, made her debut as Mimi on January 20 and later sang both Musetta and Micaela with Caruso. The versatile contralto Edyth Walker turned into a soprano during the last of her three Metropolitan seasons and sang both Amneris and Brünnhilde. Marion Weed was the first Gertrude in *Hänsel und Gretel*. Marie Rappold was cast in Lilli Lehmann's part of Sulamith in a revival of *The Queen of Sheba*. Robert Blass, the first American Gurnemanz, proved a sturdy addition to the bass section.

Nor were Americans limited to this outstanding list. The two highest paid women in the company, Emma Eames and Lillian Nordica, both came from Maine. Louise Homer, who sang the leading Wagnerian contralto roles, was a native of Pittsburgh.

Most of the training and early experience of these artists had been achieved in Europe, but they were American born, and their continued popularity in leading European opera houses gave additional prestige to the Metropolitan as an American institution.

Another prolonged spring tour was cut short in San Francisco by the momentous earthquake and fire of April 18, 1906, when the company's scenery and costumes went up in smoke in the Grand Opera House. To help make up for the personal losses of the chorus, technical staff and musicians, who had not been able to save their instruments, generous Mme. Sembrich, herself one of the chief sufferers, raised $10,000 at a benefit concert.

The management decided to refund the price of all tickets which could be produced, or whose possession could be legally established on evidence or oath. When every charred stub or half-burned wallet had been examined, every story heard and every plausible claim honored, the Metropolitan found itself short of its original intake by only a negligible amount! As a return gesture toward such an honorable public, the Metropolitan put on a mammoth benefit for the San Francisco sufferers.

It was lucky that the company added to its roster one of the most popular American singers in its history in the following season, 1906-07, for the rivalry of Oscar Hammerstein's new opera company at the Manhattan Opera House offered a fresh menace to the Metropolitan box office. Melba and Calvé both signed contracts with the competing management.

From her debut as Juliette in the opening night *Roméo* on November 23, the beautiful Geraldine Farrar was hailed for her "charming personality" and "alluring stage presence." "Her full rich soprano" voice and "dramatic quality" were further noted by the New York *Times* reviewer.

For ten years Olive Fremstad vitalized
Wagnerian heroines sometimes singing Venus
as seen here, sometimes Elisabeth.

Enrico Caruso opened the 1903 season as
the Rigoletto Duke and was featured in
every opening thereafter but one till 1920.

Within a fortnight Miss Farrar sang Marguerite in the first American stage performance of Berlioz' *Damnation of Faust* and on New Year's Eve added Gounod's Marguerite, which had been the role of her brilliant Berlin debut. On February 11 she enacted the first of her 95 Butterflys, most popular of all her Metropolitan heroines.

It is said that Farrar refused the title role of Strauss' *Salome*, the most important novelty of Conried's fourth season, which was accepted instead by Olive Fremstad. The bewildering drama was first shown at a semipublic dress rehearsal, rather tactlessly set by Mr. Conried on a Sunday, January 20. Two days later the house was crowded by an audience which had paid double prices to witness what must have attracted some of them as "a shocker." The next morning the press fulminated with "righteous fury." The Real Estate Company threatened to cancel the operating company's lease. In spite of heroic preparations and a heavy investment in the production, *Salome* was withdrawn by the management.

Two novelties were introduced to the Metropolitan repertory this season, both of which served as vehicles for Caruso and for the beautiful Lina Cavalieri, who remained with the company for two seasons. The first was Giordano's *Fedora*, in which Cavalieri made her debut on December 5. The second was Puccini's *Manon Lescaut*, which was presented on January 18, in the presence of the composer, Giacomo Puccini.

Expansion was the keynote of Conried's final Metropolitan season, 1907-08.

Geraldine Farrar created Mma. Butterfly at the Metropolitan, rapturously admired for sixteen years.

Feodor Chaliapin as Boris Godunoff, an unforgettable role he sang from 1921, though first heard in 1907.

Thursday night was added to the number of subscription series. The season was lengthened to twenty weeks. The irrepressible Caruso sang fifty-one times, or once in every three performances. Again two operas were introduced to Metropolitan audiences as vehicles for his art: Cilea's *Adriana Lecouvreur* which opened the season on November 18 and Mascagni's *Iris* which was presented on December 6. Not content with one great Italian tenor, Conried also engaged Alessandro Bonci, to apply his delicate talents to the lyric roles.

Faced with the Gallic resources of his rival, Oscar Hammerstein, the Metropolitan manager strengthened his Italian and German wings. The great Russian bass, Feodor Chaliapin, made such an impressive debut on November 20 in Boito's *Mefistofele* that the work was repeated six times. Chaliapin also sang six Basilios, three Méphistophélès in *Faust* and two Leporellos before retiring to Europe. He did not reappear at the Metropolitan for fifteen years.

The *Don Giovanni* revival was entrusted to another important newcomer of Mr. Conried's last season, the Austrian conductor, Gustav Mahler. Although the Metropolitan was accused of undue emphasis on Italian opera at this time, Mahler's influence must be cited as opening new vistas on the German repertory. His debut on January 1, 1908, conducting *Tristan und Isolde,* was celebrated by the *Tribune* as "doing honor to himself, Wagner's music and the New York public." The *Walküre* and *Fidelio* which followed, both featuring the German soprano Berta Morena, who made her debut as Sieglinde on March 4, convinced the public that Mahler was worthy to inherit the mantle of Seidl, Paur and Mottl.

In spite of the exhilaration of such artistic achievements, Heinrich Conried was a harassed and broken man. Racked by financial worries, disturbed by the constant pressure of competition from the Hammerstein forces, tortured by neuritis and even forced to come to the opera house for a while on crutches, he leaned heavily on his associate, Ernest Goerlitz. On February 11, 1908 he resigned as General Manager and announcement was official made that the company had been reorganized with Giulio Gatti-Casazza and Andreas Dippel to serve jointly as his successors.

Conried's five-year administration marks a transition between the stellar age of Maurice Grau and the later eras when dramatic personalities were sometimes sacrificed to the balance of well-rounded productions. A shrewd man of the theatre, he will go down into history for introducing such great art works as *Parsifal* and *Salome* and such sterling artists as Caruso, Farrar and Chaliapin whose overwhelming popularity grew out of their inherent worth. Constantly threatened by the keenest rivalry that the Metropolitan had had to face in twenty years and blighted by a major physical disaster, he continued to carry the operatic gospel to half a dozen cities the following spring. He fostered American singers; of Austrian birth himself, he was known for his development of Italian opera. He carried the company a long way forward on the international road.

A Quarter-Century of Gatti-Casazza

ARTISTIC FERTILITY IN THE TOSCANINI YEARS 1908-15

WITH THE ARRIVAL of Gatti-Casazza, the Metropolitan Opera Company dispensed with the name of any individual in its official title as it welcomed to its helm the first General Manager to bring a first-rate professional operatic experience as well as a cultural background to its affairs. Abbey has been described as "a purely speculative manager." He and his colleagues, Schoeffel and Grau were not averse to an evening at the gaming table, where they had earned the sobriquet "Ante, Shuffle and Grab."

Grau, trained as a lawyer, grew to be the shrewd purveyor of personalities. His early stage experience had been in operetta, concert and the spoken drama. In addition to his list of operatic celebrities he had managed Rubinstein, Wieniawski, Ristori and Offenbach. Conried as a young actor from Austria had worked himself up to manage a small German theatre in New York.

Giulio Gatti-Casazza was a university man, the son of a senator, a mathematician and naval engineer, whose life had turned to music and who had risen to a directorship at Ferrara at the age of twenty-three. For ten years he had occupied the post of General Director at La Scala in Milan, which under his management had become the leading opera house in Italy. Here he had built his career in collaboration with his colleague, Arturo Toscanini.

Ten years later the two men arrived in New York: Gatti the reticent disciplinarian, eclectic in taste, his philosophy grounded on the belief of his idol, Giuseppe Verdi, in the significance of box-office returns as "the only documents which measure success or failure"; Toscanini the sensitive and sincere artist, temperamental and intransigent, versatile in his gifts, broad as Gatti in taste, minutely scrupulous in performance.

Together the pair exerted a profound influence on operatic standards at the Metropolitan for the seven years of Toscanini's leavening influence.

When they arrived they found many artists of the company united in support of Andreas Dippel, the tenor, who, unknown to Gatti, had been appointed Administrative Manager. They were also confronted with the competition of the Hammerstein Company which had acquired the leading French artists of the day. It must be admitted that the weapons on hand for the conflict were considerable. From his predecessor Gatti had inherited Eames and Farrar, Fremstad, Homer and Sembrich, Caruso, Scotti and Campanari and the admirable conductors, Gustav Mahler and Alfred Hertz.

To this arsenal he added not only his brilliant associate Toscanini, but a score of new artists. The six who were to lend most glory to the Metropolitan were Frances Alda, the gifted lyric soprano from New Zealand who sang at the Metropolitan for over twenty years and for eighteen of them (1910-28) was the wife of the General Manager; Emmy Destinn, the great Czech soprano who sang leading dramatic roles for more than a decade; Pasquale Amato, the imaginative baritone who was still with the company at Gatti's silver jubilee in 1933; Adamo Didur, the Polish bass who created Boris Godunoff and the American bass, Herbert Witherspoon, who inherited Gatti's post as General Manager only a few weeks before his untimely death in 1935 and finally Angelo Bada, the skillful character actor and tenor buffo, who is said to have learned 150 roles during his thirty years at the Metropolitan.

A new chorus director, Giulio Setti, a new choreographer and ballet master, Ottokar Bartik, a new ballet mistress, Malvina Cavalazzi, new scenery, properties and costumes all added new lustre to the theatre.

The season opened traditionally with a performance of *Faust*, with Farrar, Caruso and Didur, but all precedents were broken by staging it in Brooklyn, where it served to open the new Academy of Music on November 14, 1908.

The gala Metropolitan opening on November 16 proved to be the first of six inaugural *Aïdas*, "a performance of exceptional splendor," according to the *Times*.

The remarkable record of new works which Gatti-Casazza was to sustain throughout his twenty-seven years, averaging four a season, was established from the year 1908-09. Of these 103 novelties, 47 did not survive their original season and only a dozen achieved anything approaching permanent place in the repertory.

By the superficial observer such facts may be taken to impugn Gatti's skill as a connoisseur of masterpieces. They can be interpreted to demonstrate the generous sweep of his experiments, which included fourteen American works.

Two of the novelties of the first season, Puccini's first opera *Le Villi* and Catalani's *La Wally*, were conducted by Toscanini. Alfred Hertz was responsible for the premiere of d'Albert's *Tiefland* on November 23, sharing responsibilities with Dippel, who supervised the production.

Emmy Destinn, who sang the title role of *La Wally*, also enacted the heroines of *Tiefland* and *The Bartered Bride*, the final and most successful novelty of the year, which was presented on the 19th of February under the direction of Mahler.

Fully as distinguished were the revivals of the year: *Le Nozze di Figaro* with Eames, Sembrich, Farrar and Scotti; *Manon*, with Farrar and Caruso; the Christmas Day performance of *L'Elisir d'Amore* with Sembrich and Bonci and Toscanini's presentation of *Falstaff* with Alda, Destinn and Scotti.

The *Ring* was deferred until a spring season, which brought the year's record to 134 performances in twenty-one weeks, followed by twenty-four performances

Lucrezia Bori, irresistible from her Manon Lescaut, 1912, to her final French Manon, 1935.

in April in Chicago and Pittsburgh as well as occasional representations in Brooklyn, Philadelphia and Baltimore.

Two important chapters in the history of the company closed toward the end of Gatti's first season. On February 6, Mme. Sembrich made her official farewell to opera, a quarter of a century after her debut on the second night of the first Metropolitan season. A week later Emma Eames sang her last Tosca on February 15, announcing that she would not again be heard in opera.

In spite of these losses to his ranks, Gatti-Casazza continued to wage aggressive and victorious battle for the supremacy of Metropolitan Opera. During his second season, 1909-10, which marked the defeat of the Hammerstein Company, the Metropolitan broke all previous boundaries in its progress.

On the night following the opening *Gioconda* of November 15, the first of a

Léon Rothier in the role
of his debut, Méphistophélès.
He sang it until 1937.

Frances Alda as Mimi. Her career was
also a long one: 1908 until 1929.

Louise Homer as Mona,
heroine of the prize
opera by Horatio Parker.

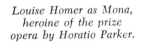

Giuseppe De Luca as Figaro,
hailed from 1915 for
"intelligence and comic power."

Giovanni Martinelli's Manrico,
lusty from 1915 to 1945.

In Frieda Hempel "the opera has
gained greatly," wrote the Times.

series of semiweekly performances was offered at The New Theatre, where the young soprano, Alma Gluck and the lyric French tenor, Edmond Clément made their debuts in *Werther,* with Farrar taking Eames' original role of Charlotte. This experiment endured for a single season only, but enabled the public to hear a variety of lighter operas, sung by Metropolitan artists.

Two of the five novelties of the season, Auber's *Fra Diavolo* and Flotow's *Stradella,* were chosen as appropriate to the auditorium of The New Theatre. Another, Franchetti's *Germania,* provided Caruso's only new role of the year.

Tchaikovsky's *Pique Dame,* presented in German on March 5 under the direction of Mahler, with Leo Slezak, the company's new Moravian dramatic tenor, as Hermann, was the first Russian opera to be offered at the Metropolitan.

An equally momentous precedent was set by the management in the first American opera to be offered in the theatre, Frederic Converse's *The Pipe of Desire,* which was sung on March 18 under the baton of Alfred Hertz by an all-American cast: the young Kentucky tenor, Riccardo Martin, Louise Homer, Clarence Whitehill and Herbert Witherspoon.

Another innovation was the engagement of two great Russian dancers, Anna Pavlowa and Mikhail Mordkin, whose ballets brightened the repertory.

In the spring of 1910 two important events in Metropolitan history were brought about largely through the initiative of Otto H. Kahn, who had become president of the producing company in 1908. One was the purchase of all Oscar Hammerstein's contracts and properties except the Manhattan Opera House, for $1,200,000 and the subsequent organization of the Chicago-Philadelphia Grand Opera Company under Andreas Dippel. Thus the Hammerstein rivalry was

Emmy Destinn, seen here as Senta in The Flying Dutchman, *brought a powerful, dramatic voice to the Opera House from her 1908 Aïda to Nedda in 1920.*

Pasquale Amato was chosen for the Sheriff at the world premiere of Puccini's Girl of the Golden West. *He made a convincing villain for twenty-five years.*

eliminated, while an interlocking directorate assured the development of opera in Chicago, Philadelphia, Boston and New York under central control.

An even broader field was reached on May 21, when the Metropolitan Company opened a brief season at the Châtelet Theatre in Paris, where Lucrezia Bori made her debut with her future colleagues in *Manon Lescaut*, opposite Caruso.

Two leading composers attended the world premieres of their operas during the 1910-11 season at the Metropolitan Opera House. On December 10, Giacomo Puccini first witnessed his *Girl of the Golden West* with Destinn, Caruso and Amato and described the performance, which was led by Toscanini, as "perfect."

On December 28 Engelbert Humperdinck was on hand to applaud Geraldine Farrar in her creation of the Goose-Girl in *Königskinder*.

Nor did Gatti neglect the classic repertory. On opening night he offered Gluck's *Armide* under the baton of Toscanini, who had presented a magnificent *Orfeo* the year before with Gadski, Homer and Gluck. The latter artists participated in the Metropolitan premiere of *Armide* with Caruso and Fremstad.

The last novelty of the season was Dukas' *Ariane et Barbe Bleu* on March 29, also under Toscanini. The title roles were taken by Farrar and the French bass, Léon Rothier, who had initiated a long career as Méphistophélès.

If none of the novelties offered during the season of 1911-12 was of enduring influence on the repertory, the one American composition, Horatio Parker's *Mona,* represented a serious ambition to further a national art. It had been awarded a $10,000 prize offered by the company two years before and was conducted on March 14 by Mr. Hertz with Riccardo Martin and Louise Homer.

Another excursion into the classic field was effected in a concert version of Monteverdi's *Orfeo* on April 14.

The Wagnerian repertory profited much this season from the engagement of Margarete Matzenauer, who sang twelve contralto and two soprano roles, opening a career which endured for nearly twenty years..

The Lucias and Gildas formerly sung by Sembrich, now fell to Luisa Tetrazzini, who made her debut on December 27 as Donizetti's ill-fated heroine.

Again this year Pavlowa and Mordkin offered their ballets and *divertissements.* Again Enrico Caruso, whose illness during the preceding winter had reduced his Metropolitan appearances, sang over forty performances with the company, including twelve *Pagliaccis.* Again the Metropolitan concluded a brief spring tour in Atlanta, where it played seven performances in April and was given such a royal welcome that it repeated its visit to the city each spring with a single interruption, for twenty-seven years.

The season of 1912-13 reached new dimensions in the internationalism of its novelties and revivals, a new distinction in the quality of its artists.

The first of these to appear was Lucrezia Bori, who was honored with the title role of *Manon Lescaut* on opening night, November 11, with a new conductor, Giorgio Polacco, on the podium, opposite Caruso and Scotti. Miss Bori at once displayed a captivating instinct for comedy, a gift for pathos and "an intimate knowledge of the uses of the voice." From her first season these were evidenced in her Nedda, Mimi, Antonia and Norina, under Sturani and Polacco.

Under the latter maestro Frieda Hempel made her debut as Marguerite de Valois in a revival of *Les Huguenots* on December 27, when she was heard with Destinn, Alten, Caruso, Scotti, Didur and Rothier.

Bad luck seemed to haunt the Wagnerian singers. The new tenor, Jacques Urlus, lost his voice at his debut in *Tristan*. A similar calamity befell Hermann Weil, a baritone who went hoarse in the *Meistersinger* second act riot.

Meanwhile the four novelties were assigned to a variety of conductors. Polacco introduced Wolf-Ferrari's miniature *Segreto di Susanna* on December 13 with Farrar and Scotti. He also presided at the first production of *Les Contes D'Hoffmann* in which Bori was joined by Hempel as Olympia and Fremstad as Giulietta with Umberto Macnez as Hoffmann. Alfred Hertz was entrusted as usual with the new American work, Walter Damrosch's *Cyrano de Bergerac*, presented on February 27 in an English version which William J. Henderson, critic of the New York *Sun*, had made from Rostand"s play. Amato, Alda and Martin sang the leading roles.

The most significant premiere of the season, however, was *Boris Godunoff*, which was directed by Toscanini on the 19th of March. The scenery and costumes had been purchased in Paris, rich in the authentic designs and colors devised by a group of Russian artists at the command of the Czar. The impress of the conductor's "master hand and the certainty of his touch" were noted by the *Times* reviewer, while all agreed on the "remarkably vivid and dramatically thrilling impersonation" of the remorseful Emperor by Adamo Didur. The debut of Paul Althouse, a sturdy tenor from Reading, Pennsylvania, was hailed for the "unusual beauty" of his vocal quality.

Der Rosenkavalier and *L'Amore dei tre re* have been called the last two masterworks which have appeared on the European horizon. Both of them were introduced into the Metropolitan repertory by Gatti-Casazza during the last of his pre-war seasons. The Strauss-von Hofmannsthal comedy was presented on December 9 under Alfred Hertz' direction with a cast led by Frieda Hempel, Margarete Ober, a new mezzo soprano of the season who had been recognized at once as a talented actress, and the handsome young American Anna Case as Sophie with Otto Goritz as Baron Ochs.

L'Amore dei tre re, which was offered on January 2 with much less fanfare, gained immeasurably from the poetical interpretation of Toscanini and the flower-like delineation of the heroine by Lucrezia Bori as well as the eloquence of the passionate young hero, sung by the new Italian tenor, Edoardo Ferrari-Fontana. Adamo Didur interpreted the ancient Archibaldo.

Another addition to the tenor ranks this season was Giovanni Martinelli who on November 20 as Rodolfo, with Bori as his Mimi, opened a career which was to last for thirty years at the theatre.

44

On the other side of the ledger this year was the withdrawal of Olive Frem-stad, who sang her final Elsa on April 23.

A gala performance of *Un Ballo in Maschera* opened the 1914-15 season on November 16, with the same cast as in its revival the previous year: Destinn, Hempel, Matzenauer, Caruso, Rothier, Amato and Segurola, a brilliant assembly of stars gathered under the baton of Toscanini in what was to prove his final season at the Metropolitan.

After a five-year lapse *Carmen* was soon revived for Geraldine Farrar, with Caruso, Amato and Alda, also under Toscanini, with Désiré Defrère, the present Metropolitan stage director, making his debut as Morales and Rosina Galli appearing for the first time as *première danseuse*.

Two new singers were added to the Wagnerian wing, Melanie Kurt, who made her debut as Isolde on February 1 and Johannes Sembach, who sang his initial *Parsifal* at the Thanksgiving Day matinee.

The novelties of the season included the world premiere of *Madame Sans Gêne*, Giordano's animated version of Sardou's Napoleonic drama, in which Geraldine Farrar was featured and Leoni's brief melodrama of Chinatown, *L'Oracolo*, which proved an ideal vehicle for Antonio Scotti's macabre talents until his farewell in the role of Chim-Fen, nearly twenty years later. *L'Oracolo* was conducted by Polacco, *Sans Gêne* by Toscanini, who was also responsible for the revival of Weber's *Euryanthe*, which had not been heard for nearly a quarter of a century and for a restudied *Trovatore* with new scenery. Among the maestro's final assignments were *Meistersinger, Carmen* and *Iris*, which he led on April 14 with Bori, Didur, Luca Botta and Scotti, the last of the twenty-nine operas which he had illumined with his sensitive insight and electric vitality.

THE INFLUENCE OF THE FIRST WORLD WAR 1915-21

World War I did not prevent Gatti-Casazza from adding three distinguished foreign artists in the winter of 1915-16. First of these to appear at the Opera House was Artur Bodanzky, the Viennese conductor who made his debut on the third night of the season. His interpretation of *Götterdämmerung* on November 18 at once showed the vitality and precision of his art and also disclosed his practice of cutting the Wagner music dramas in the interests of increased public enjoyment. The renaissance of the Wagnerian cult, especially in the last years of his Metropolitan career, cut short by his death at the outset of his twenty-fifth season, must in part be credited to his stirring performances.

A week after Bodanzky's debut a new Italian lyric baritone, Giuseppe De Luca, founded an enduring artistic reputation at the Metropolitan with his first Figaro in the November 25 *Barber*.

Additional proof that the art of *bel canto* had not disappeared from the stage was given by Maria Barrientos, the Spanish coloratura soprano, who made a deep impression for thorough musicianship and an exotic and engaging personality in her first *Lucia* on January 31.

A heritage from Arturo Toscanini, who had left the United States the preceding spring, as Gatti explained "because of his interest in the War," was one of the most interesting novelties of the season, Borodin's *Prince Igor.* This was introduced on December 30 with Frances Alda, Luca Botta and Pasquale Amato, having been prepared by Toscanini before his departure.

The production of Granados' *Goyescas,* an opera which had been woven out of a number of the composer's familiar piano pieces, brought the war even nearer home. It was not only the first Spanish work to be presented at the Metropolitan in the language of Spain, which remained neutral in the conflict, but it aroused sufficient public interest in the composer to fill the house when a benefit concert was arranged in May to help the family of Granados, who had been lost at sea on his return journey with his wife, when the S.S. *Sussex* was torpedoed by the enemy.

Another highlight of the season was the restudied *Rigoletto,* for which new settings were provided and which set a precedent later developed by Edward Johnson of entrusting revivals of standard works to new conductors and rehearsing them as if they were novelties.

The influence of cinema technique on operatic stars was quoted this year by the critics, who reviewed a vigorous performance of *Carmen* on February 17, when Farrar, who had recently made her melodramatic screen *Carmen* with Wallace Reid, had a spectacular scuffle with Caruso. The press also ran wild!

The reduction of the season to twenty weeks may be cited as evidence of wartime difficulties. It was utilized, however, by the engagement of the Diaghileff Ballet during the month of April, with Nijinsky as leading star.

At the close of the season Gatti's contract was renewed for three years and Edward Ziegler was added to the staff as Administrative Secretary.

War shadows fell more sharply across the season of 1916-17, when during a performance of Reginald DeKoven's *Canterbury Pilgrims,* the American novelty of the year, word was brought that President Wilson had asked Congress to declare a state of war. Bodanzky conducted "The Star Spangled Banner." Margarete Ober, who had been playing the Wife of Bath, fainted on the stage. Soon Johanna Gadski, whose husband had represented the Krupp munition works, withdrew from the Metropolitan.

The entry of the United States into the conflict took place on Good Friday, but *Parsifal* was not canceled and opera in German continued as usual through the last of the twenty-three weeks, in accordance with the expressed desire of the General Manager to continue the practice.

Indeed the outstanding novelty of the season had been the performance in German of Gluck's *Iphigenia auf Tauris,* in the version prepared by Richard Strauss and now interpreted by Bodanzky on November 25. This was offered with Melanie Kurt in the title role, Sembach as Pylades and Marie Sundelius making her debut as the first priestess.

The absence of Lucrezia Bori, who had been forced by a vocal affliction to retire the year before, necessitated the engagement of another leading soprano.

46

On December 4 dramatic Claudia Muzio, the brilliant daughter of an assistant stage manager of the company, made her debut as Tosca, with Caruso and Scotti. The popularity of the tenor also accounted for the revival of *L'Elisir d'Amore* on December 30, under the baton of Gennaro Papi, who had been promoted this season to conductorial rank.

For Miss Farrar, Massenet's *Thaïs* was introduced into the Metropolitan repertory on February 16 with Amato as Athanael, Polacco conducting.

During the following season, 1917-18, the war made its mark increasingly felt on operatic affairs. Five Wagnerian singers departed: Kurt, Ober, Sembach, Braun and Goritz. Public prejudice against the German language grew so heated that no German operas were given.

Instead Gatti offered Liszt's oratorio *Saint Elizabeth* in an operatic English version by Constance Bache. The Hungarian origin and international background of the composer warded off unfavorable comment. The American public had not yet decided that the elimination of works by composers from enemy countries might be interpreted as a form of defeatism.

And so the General Manager offered one Italian, one American, one French and one Russian work, which proved to be the most enduring of the four. This was Rimsky-Korsakoff's *Coq d'Or*, which was introduced on March 6 with Didur and Barrientos singing the roles of King and Queen from bleachers at the sides of the stage and Adolph Bolm and Rosina Galli dancing and miming the parts.

Next most popular was Rabaud's *Marouf*, in which Alda and De Luca sang leading roles at the American premiere on December 19.

Both of these operas were led by Pierre Monteux, the new conductor of the season, who had made his debut in an important revival of *Faust* on November 17 with Farrar, Martinelli and Rothier in the cast and new sets by Josef Urban, the first in a long series of imaginative stage designs.

Another distinguished scenic artist, Norman Bel Geddes, embellished the premiere of Charles Wakefield Cadman's *Shanewis* on March 23, when Sophie Braslau sang the title role and Roberto Moranzoni, another newcomer of the season, conducted. Other interesting debuts of the season were those of John McCormack, who first appeared as a regular member of the company in the

Claudia Muzio did not sing Violetta till 1934, when the beautiful soprano returned after ten years' absence.

47

November 16 *Bohème* and Florence Easton, who on December 7 sang Santuzza, her first Metropolitan role, which led the way to many rich-voiced and nobly conceived interpretations.

The elation of the Armistice pervaded the opening night of the season of 1918-19, when the flags of the Allies were massed on the stage during an intermission of *Samson et Dalila* on November 11.

Four days later the young American dramatic soprano, Rosa Ponselle, made a deep impression at her debut in *La Forza del Destino,* which entered the Metropolitan repertory on November 15 under Papi's baton with Caruso and De Luca. She also appeared in a novelty of the season, Weber's *Oberon,* which had been prepared in an abbreviated form by Artur Bodanzky and was offered in English on December 28 with Paul Althouse in the title role.

Another Puccini world premiere was offered at the Metropolitan on December 14: the trilogy of one-act operas of which *Gianni Schicchi* still adds its wit and vivacity to the repertory. This was interpreted by De Luca with Florence Easton as Lauretta. Claudia Muzio acted as heroine of the brief melodrama *Il Tabarro,* which opened the program, and Farrar played the title role in the picture of convent life, *Suor Angelica.* Two brief American novelties. Breil's *Legend* and Hugo's *Temple Dancer* shared another triple bill with *Shanewis.*

News interest also centered in the opera house in March, when Caruso celebrated his twenty-fifth anniversary on the 22nd with a series of operatic scenes from *L'Elisir d'Amore, Pagliacci* and *Le Prophète.* At the tenor's request, the proceeds were turned over to the Emergency Fund of the Metropolitan.

Among the new artists of the season were two Americans, the tenor, Charles Hackett from Worcester, Mass., and the Brooklyn baritone, Reinald Werrenrath.

Wagner returned to the Metropolitan in the season of 1919-20 by way of an English version of *Parsifal,* by Henry E. Krehbiel, presented on February 19 with an international cast which did not include a single German. Its record of six performances had not been surpassed since the first Conried seasons. New settings were designed for the occasion by Josef Urban and the moving scenery was replaced by a curtain painted with mystic figures.

Of the season's five novelties, Leoncavallo's *Zaza* held the stage longest, proving a popular instrument for Geraldine Farrar's dynamic personality for three years and finally serving as the vehicle of her farewell. It was cast with Amato and Kathleen Howard, a Canadian contralto who had won praise for her keen characterizations since her debut, three years before.

Of greater news value, however, was the world premiere of Albert Wolff's *Blue Bird,* which had been conducted by the composer on December 27, with the poet Maeterlinck and his wife in attendance.

Another headline event was the gala tendered to the Prince of Wales on November 18, when the leading members of the company sang operatic excerpts.

On March 24 Gatti offered the New York stage premiere of Tchaikovsky's *Eugen Onegin* in an Italian version, although the work was directed by Artur

Bodanzky with Muzio, Martinelli and DeLuca in the leading roles.

Halévy's *La Juive,* which had not been heard at the Opera House for thirty years, was restored on November 22 for Caruso and was joyously recognized as the crowning dramatic effort of the tenor's career. Ponselle was accorded the title role, while the Indiana tenor, Orville Harrold, made his debut as Leopold. Artur Bodanzky was in charge of the production.

The season of 1920-21 was the last in which the German language was banished from the opera house as a result of wartime prejudice. *Tristan* was restored on November 20 in an English translation by H. & F. Corder, revised by Sigmund Spaeth and Cecil Cowdry with Matzenauer and Sembach; *Lohengrin* on February 2 with Easton and Sembach, both conducted by Bodanzky with new sets by Urban.

An irreparable loss was this year sustained by the Metropolitan in the illness of Enrico Caruso who suffered a hemorrhage during a performance of *Pagliacci* on December 8, was forced to withdraw from a Brooklyn performance of *L'Elisir d'Amore* on December 11 and sang a total of only eight performances in the Opera House before his final *La Juive* on December 24. On Christmas Day he collapsed from what was then diagnosed as pleurisy and died the following August 2nd in Naples.

In the 607 performances which Caruso had contributed to the glories of the Metropolitan, he had developed the natural *bel canto* of his brilliant tenor voice into a powerful dramatic organ, darker in color than when it first sounded, but now based on a chastened artistry capable of deep emotional characterizations. His recordings won him a world-wide public and served to inspire young singers in every corner of the globe. His nature in its turn had developed from the impishness of prolonged adolescence into the courageous, generous and lovable personality of a great man. The Metropolitan Opera family staggered under his loss.

A month before Caruso's final performance, a new lyric tenor presented himself as Faust in Boito's *Mefistofele* on November 26. This was Beniamino Gigli, who inherited many of his great predecessor's earlier roles. In the place of Caruso, Gigli was also cast in the title role of *Andrea Chenier,* which was introduced for the first time to Metropolitan audiences on March 7 and held the stage for thirteen consecutive years. Its premiere was cast with Claudia Muzio and Giuseppe Danise, a talented dramatic baritone who had made his debut as Amonasro on November 17.

The Opera House enjoyed another saving grace this season in the return of Lucrezia Bori, after five years of illness, convalescence and additional preparation for her reappearance. At her first Mimi on January 28, with Gigli and Scotti, the Spanish soprano was welcomed with an avalanche of flowers.

Two Metropolitan novelties, garnished with new settings by Josef Urban, provided interesting roles for two other leading sopranos of the company. On December 23 Verdi's *Don Carlos* was introduced with Ponselle, Matzenauer, Martinelli, De Luca and Didur in a strong cast under Papi's baton.

On January 15 Albert Wolff conducted the first *Louise* in the history of the company, with Geraldine Farrar in the title role.

If no tenor could be found of the stature of Enrico Caruso; two sopranos, a baritone and a bass brought renown to the Opera House in 1921-22.

In the opening night *Traviata* on November 14, the mellow coloratura of Amelita Galli-Curci was heard in the theatre for the first time. With Gigli and De Luca she was now seen in a new and luxurious setting by Josef Urban.

The first week also introduced the Austrian dramatic soprano, Maria Jeritza, whose dazzling blonde beauty was first applauded in the American premiere of Korngold's *Die Tote Stadt* on November 19. A few weeks later Jeritza sang her first Tosca and won especial attention by opening her *Vissi d'arte* lying prone upon the floor. The grim melodrama of Bruges also served to present a Minneapolis tenor, George Meader, who sang effective character parts for several years.

The return of Feodor Chaliapin was hailed in *Boris Godunoff* on December 9, when he sang the title role in its original tongue with the Italian ensemble.

The third important debut was that of the Italian baritone, Titta Ruffo, who came to the Metropolitan as Figaro on January 19.

Tristan and *Die Walküre* both re-entered the repertory this season in German. *Parsifal*, however, was retained in English, while *Lohengrin* was sung by Jeritza in German, with the chorus clinging to English.

Two charming heroines with the features of Lucrezia Bori were first applauded by Metropolitan audiences this season. On January 23 Rimsky-Korsakoff's *Snowmaiden* achieved its American premiere with the imaginative settings of Boris Anisfeld. Artur Bodanzky was also responsible for the production of *Cosi fan tutte* with Easton and Peralta as the flirtatious heroines and Bori as their sprightly maid Despina.

The French repertory, which was enriched by Lalo's *Le Roi d'Ys* on January 5 under Albert Wolff's baton, was further developed this year by a new Parisian conductor, Louis Hasselmans, who now led *Faust, Carmen, Manon* and other works at the beginning of his fourteen years of service.

At the last matinee of the season on April 22, Geraldine Farrar made a spectacular farewell as the heroine of *Zaza*, followed to the street by a brigade of some 500 "Gerryflappers," as William J. Henderson had christened her youthful adherents. Banners and confetti were mingled with tears in this emotional demonstration on behalf of one of the most magnetic of American sopranos.

The growing popularity of Maria Jeritza accounted for her assignment to the title role of *Tosca* in the opening night of the season of 1922-23, opposite Martinelli and Scotti.

It was Bori, however, who was honored in one of the two novelties of the year, Vittadini's sunny *Anima Allegra*, which was presented on February 14 with the brilliant Roman, Giacomo Lauri-Volpi, singing one tenor role and the other introducing a young Bulgarian, Armand Tokatyan.

The other new work of the winter was Max Schilling's *Mona Lisa,* which was introduced by Bodanzky on March 1, with Barbara Kemp, wife of the composer, making the first of her scant number of appearances with the company in the title role. The dramatic personality of the German bass, Michael Bohnen, was also first applauded in this opera.

More familiar roles served as the debut vehicles for other artists who stood up well under the inevitable comparisons. On November 16 a handsome, youthful and sympathetic Avito was welcomed to *L'Amore dei tre re.* This was Edward Johnson, whose "fine voice and manly bearing . . . earned him a warm reception."

In the November 22 *Aïda,* both Elisabeth Rethberg and Sigrid Onegin made their first Metropolitan appearance and were appraised as exceptionally gifted artists, winning applause for the purity and richness of their tone.

Urban's new sets for *Butterfly* embellished the tragedy in which Easton was presented while Bori was wooed against his new background for *Roméo.*

In 1923-24 the Metropolitan opera season reached its maximum duration of twenty-four weeks, which it retained for nine consecutive years.

Although the opening night was again consecrated to Maria Jeritza in a performance of Massenet's *Thaïs,* the season was especially noteworthy for the development of the German repertory. This included a revival of *Meistersinger* in which the personable tenor Rudolf Laubenthal made his debut, Easton shared soprano responsibilities with Rethberg and Whitehill returned to his distinguished impersonation of Hans Sachs. This role was soon to be shared in its turn with Friedrich Schorr, the renowned Hungarian baritone who made his Metropolitan debut on February 14, replacing Whitehill as Wolfram.

Another valued addition to the Wagnerian wing was the Swedish contralto and mezzo-soprano Karin Branzell, who offered her first Fricka in the February 6

The "high, clear, liquid tones" of Elisabeth Rethberg's 1922 Aïda delighted the Times.

Beniamino Gigli sang des Grieux in the operas of both Jules Massenet and Giacomo Puccini.

Walküre but miraculously sang Brünnhilde in the same work on March 17.

Less significant to all immediate appearances was the debut of the California baritone, Lawrence Tibbett, who was first assigned to the minor role of the Jesuit Lovitzki in *Boris* on November 24 but rose rapidly the following year.

Meanwhile Antonio Scotti rounded out a quarter-century at the Metropolitan in a gala performance of *Tosca* on New Year's Day with Maria Jeritza in the title role and nearly $20,000 in the house.

The spring tour was this year extended to include two performances in Rochester and seven in Cleveland, where the Civic Auditorium was completed, enabling nine thousand music lovers to witness opera in a single night.

One novelty of the 1924-25 season was Debussy's *Pelléas et Mélisande,* presented on March 21, when Lucrezia Bori and Edward Johnson achieved what Lawrence Gilman in the *Herald Tribune* called "a memorable performance" under Louis Hasselmans' baton, repeated in the following ten seasons.

One of the most spectacular testimonials of public approval ever demonstrated at the Opera House was accorded at the revival of *Falstaff* on January 2, when the audience frantically called back Lawrence Tibbett to the stage after his impressive delivery of Ford's Monologue. The title role was taken by Antonio Scotti, who did not realize that the applause was meant for his younger colleague until it had risen to an ovation for Tibbett, who was marked for greater things.

Falstaff also served to measure the lofty musical stature of Tullio Serafin, the Venetian conductor who made his debut in the opening night *Aïda.* A revival of *Gioconda* on November 8 again demonstrated Serafin's vital art.

Brief but interesting contributions were this year added to the Wagnerian repertory by the dramatic Swedish soprano, Nanny Larsen-Todsen, the lyric soprano Maria Müller and Berta Morena, who returned after an absence of more than thirteen years to sing Brünnhilde on April 3.

Two debuts made history in the season 1925-26. On the afternoon of February 17, the Danish *Heldentenor* Lauritz Melchior sang Tannhäuser, the first in a long series of majestic Wagnerian roles. Whatever fanfare might have attended the event, which proved momentous in the subsequent development of Wagnerian music drama at the Metropolitan, was eclipsed by the publicity attending the debut of Marion Talley, a nineteen-year-old coloratura from Kansas City, who sang her first Gilda on the evening of the same day before a vociferous audience.

After four years of occasional Lucias, Olympias, Philines, Nightingales and Queens of the Night, Miss Talley retired to artistic obscurity. Melchior rose to glories in inverse proportion to the unobtrusiveness of his debut.

The varied gifts of the Metropolitan Company were further exposed in a generous list of novelties and revivals. Ponselle and Johnson were featured in the leading roles of Spontini's *La Vestale* on November 12; Jeritza sang the heroine of the *Jewels of the Madonna* on December 12 and Bori the central figures in both Falla's *Vida Breve* and Ravel's *L'Heure Espagnole,* which shared a double

Genuine theatrical value was credited to Lawrence Tibbett for the Scarpia he first portrayed in 1935.

Karin Branzell was praised for the opulence of her voice and the authority of her presence as Ortrud.

For nine years Amelita Galli-Curci sang leading coloratura roles at the Opera House. This is Rosina.

Friedrich Schorr for twenty years brought dignity and eloquence to such baritone roles as Hans Sachs.

bill with *The Barber of Bagdad* on November 7. Tibbett inherited Ruffo's share in Giordano's melodrama *La cena delle beffe,* playing with Gigli and Alda. Chaliapin found a vehicle in the picaresque hero of Massenet's *Don Quichotte.*

For ten years Gatti-Casazza had found no American opera for the Metropolitan. On February 19, 1926, he offered John Alden Carpenter's ballet, *Skyscrapers,* under Hasselmans' baton. This was repeated four times, sharing the bill in turn with *Gianni Schicchi, The Bartered Bride, Pagliacci* and *Freischütz.*

A year later Deems Taylor's opera, *The King's Henchman* was introduced, a climax of the sesaon of 1926-27. Provided with an eloquent libretto by Edna St. Vincent Millay and settings by Josef Urban, skillfully cast with Easton as the Saxon heroine Aelfrida, Tibbett as King Eadgar and Johnson as the lover Aethelwold, the new work was presented on February 17 with Serafin on the podium. The opera was hailed as "the most expert score" yet written by an American. Its fourteen performances were applauded for three seasons.

Serafin and Urban had also been occupied in ·the American premiere of Puccini's spectacular *Turandot,* which was presented on November 16, with Jeritza in the title role, and endured for four seasons.

Of future significance in Metropolitan history was the debut of Ezio Pinza on the opening night of the season on November 1, in a performance of *La Vestale* with Ponselle and Lauri-Volpi. Another artist to initiate a long and valued career this season was George Cehanovsky, who made his debut as Kothner in *Die Meistersinger* on November 13.

Bori's new role of the season was Mignon, which was heard in French on March 10 and remained steadily in the repertory after its twenty-year absence.

The world-wide boom in economic affairs was reflected in the season of 1927-28 at the Metropolitan by new highs in the prices of the ticket speculators, and new glitter in the opening night *Turandot* on October 31.

Rosa Ponselle revived interest in such dramatic roles as Norma, which was new to her generation.

Effervescent Grace Moore as Mimi, role of the soprano's debut in 1928 and return in 1936.

*Giacomo Lauri-Volpi as
Prince Calaf and Maria Jeritza
in the title role of Puccini's
Turandot, at the first American
performance, November, 1926.*

*Lauritz Melchior, photographed at a
thrilling climax in the first act of
Tristan und Isolde in perhaps the
finest role of his operatic career.*

The most important revival of the year was Bellini's *Norma* with Ponselle as the Druid Priestess and Marion Telva, the St. Louis contralto, singing Adalgisa in one of the most important assignments of her decade at the Metropolitan. Ezio Pinza was again cast as a High Priest, while Lauri-Volpi's Pollione was eventually replaced by Frederick Jagel, the versatile New York tenor who had made his Metropolitan debut on November 8 as Radames.

The American premiere of Puccini's *La Rondine* on March 10 gave Lucrezia Bori another sympathetic and vivacious role under Vincenzo Bellezza, who had arrived the year before to share the Italian repertory with Serafin.

The grand opera debut of Grace Moore as Mimi brought the two senators from Tennessee to the opera house on February 7, together with several thousand other enthusiasts. The blonde soprano quickly proved that her early musical comedy experiences had not injured the natural beauty of her voice, but helped to develop an appealing stage presence.

1928-29, the final season of the stock market boom, gained new interest from four new operas by contemporary European composers: Richard Strauss, Ernst Krenek, Ildebrando Pizzetti and Ottorino Respighi, of which only the latter's *Campana Sommersa* survived into a second season.

More acceptable to the public were revivals of *Ernani* with Ponselle, Martinelli and Ruffo; *Manon*, with Bori, Scotti and the California tenor Mario Chamlee, who had been of useful service to the company since 1920, and *Der Freischütz*, with Bohnen, Laubenthal and Müller.

The further development of the Wagnerian repertory was advanced by the return of Lauritz Melchior, after a year's absence. In March the tenor sang his first *Götterdämmerung* Siegfried in New York and his first Metropolitan Tristan, both of which added to the stature of Wagnerian tradition at the Opera House.

It was lucky that the Wall Street crash of October, 1929 followed the opening of the 1929-30 opera season by a single day, for the capacity audience which greeted Bori, Gigli and DeLuca in *Manon Lescaut* on October 28 would hardly have been in a festive mood had the market tumbled the day before. Lucky also, perhaps, that the season's subscriptions were long since paid — at the highest price yet know in Metropolitan history — $8.25 for an orchestra seat.

The most elaborate production of the season was accorded to Rimsky-Korsakoff's fantastic opera, *Sadko*, which was introduced to the American public in French on January 25 with Edward Johnson in the title role and imaginative settings by Serge Soudeikine. The heroine was played by Editha Fleischer, the German soprano who had lent animation to lyric roles since 1926.

Less significant in the future repertory of the theatre but fully as important in its historic record was the first Metropolitan performance on December 21 of Verdi's *Luisa Miller*, with Ponselle, Lauri-Volpi and De Luca, just eighty years after its premiere in Naples.

The later popularity of Gladys Swarthout, the handsome mezzo soprano from

Missouri, had small chance to be demonstrated at her debut as La Cieca in the *Gioconda* of November 15, but her art developed gradually through a series of modest roles, while she made ready for later triumphs.

Jeritza was meanwhile featured in a revival of *The Girl of the Golden West* on November 2, with new settings by Joseph Novak; and Bori in the *Louise* of March 1, while Gigli and Pinza helped to revive *L'Elisir d'Amore* on March 21.

The economic depression was flouted by the record-breaking public which flocked to the first series of uncut performances of *The Ring of the Nibelung* since 1899. Bodanzky directed a strong cast: Kappel, Branzell, Melchior, Bohnen, Schützendorf and an additional new soprano, Elizabeth Ohms.

The spring tour this season reached its maximum extension under Gatti-Casazza, with twenty-five performances in six cities in addition to the twenty-two performances played during the winter in Philadelphia.

The financial reserve which had been built up under Gatti's shrewd management stood the company in good stead during the season of 1930-31, although the depression could not yet be said to have affected the gala opening night *Aïda*.

Four novelties were lavished on the repertory, including Moussorgsky's *Fair at Sorochintzky*, but none proved so enduring as Deems Taylor's *Peter Ibbetson*, which the composer had written while enjoying a grant from the Juilliard Foundation. This nostalgic romance was effectively portrayed by Bori and Johnson, with Lawrence Tibbett as the villainous Colonel, and held the Metropolitan stage for longer than any other American work had done in the past.

A particularly bright star made her appearance in the storm-clouded firmament when Lily Pons sang her first Lucia on January 3 and without fanfare made a place for herself among the great coloratura sopranos in the history of the theatre. Each of her subsequent impersonations during the season: Gilda, Rosina, Olympia and Philine, attracted a large and more appreciative audience.

The inevitable decline of opera subscriptions in the season of 1931-32 did not appear to affect the gala opening night *Traviata* of November 2 with Ponselle, Lauri-Volpi and De Luca. Financial pressure was evident, however, in the General Manager's announcement that a cut in salary had been proposed to the employees of the company and loyally accepted by practically the entire roster.

To the depression, moreover, one major development in operatic history must be credited. For several years Gatti-Casazza had frowned on any attempt to dispense the services of his company by means of the experimental devices of the radio. Now at last he succumbed to the overtures of the National Broadcasting Company. On Christmas Day, 1931, the first Metropolitan performance was broadcast: a matinee of *Hänsel und Gretel* with Editha Fleischer and Queena Mario in the title roles, Dorothee Manski as the Witch and Riedel on the podium. Deems Taylor was the commentator, Milton Cross, the announcer.

Another chapter in the administration of the Metropolitan was now opened. Heralded by the resignation of Otto H. Kahn, who had presided over the affairs of the producing company for more than twenty years and the announcement that he would be replaced by Paul D. Cravath, a reorganization was effected. On November 21, 1932, the Metropolitan Opera Association, Inc. was formed.

Even under financial stress, however, Gatti's repertory was further expanded in the season of 1931-32. Outstanding for the impressive interpretation of Lawrence Tibbett in the title role, Verdi's *Simon Boccanegra* was presented on January 28 under Bellezza's baton, a high artistic achievement.

Artur Bodanzky was responsible for the premiere of Weinberger's *Schwanda*, with Friedrich Schorr in the title role, and also for *Donna Juanita*, another von Suppé operetta for Maria Jeritza, to follow her earlier success in *Boccaccio*.

Revivals of *Lakmé* on February 19 and *La Sonnambula* on March 16 gave further scope to the delicate art of Lily Pons, while on December 2 Ponselle appeared in the title role of Montemezzi's *La Notte di Zoraima*.

The first reduction in prices in nearly fifty years indicated the management's inevitable response to the depression in the season of 1932-33, which was also contracted to sixteen weeks, the shortest period since the days of Conried.

Soon after the opening night *Boccanegra* on November 21, new artists were presented to the public. On the second night the Italian tenor Tito Schipa made his debut as Nemorino in *L'Elisir d'Amore*. A few days later a German baritone, Ludwig Hofmann, and an American, Richard Bonelli, added power to the Wagnerian and lyric Italian repertories. On November 28 Rose Bampton, a statuesque mezzo soprano from Cleveland, made her appearance as Laura in *La Gioconda*, while Richard Crooks sang his first smooth des Grieux in a matinee of *Manon* on February 25.

It was on this same afternoon that the radio audience was first invited to participate in a nation-wide drive for $300,000 to assure the continued production of opera. Lucrezia Bori, Edward Johnson and Lawrence Tibbett were selected from the company to further the cause. Geraldine Farrar emerged from retirement to add her eloquence to the appeal. The Juilliard Foundation and the Carnegie Corporation made contributions to the fund and at a gala Opera Ball on April 27, Miss Bori announced that the quota had been reached.

Meanwhile the slender resources of the remaining Metropolitan reserves were shrewdly applied to three new productions. On December 3 "a remarkably vital performance" of Richard Strauss' *Elektra* introduced the macabre but powerful work under the baton of Artur Bodanzky with Gertrude Kappel in the title role.

A month later *The Emperor Jones*, the first play of Eugene O'Neill to reach the opera stage, was enacted by Lawrence Tibbett and his colleagues, while Gruenberg's effective score was led by Serafin with such success that the opera was heard seven times in its first season and repeated the following year. The Italian conductor also presided at the Metropolitan premiere of Rossini's *Signor Bruschino*, with Fleischer, Tokatyan, Pinza and De Luca in leading roles.

A capacity audience thronged the house for Scotti's farewell in *L'Oracolo* on January 20, crowning the baritone's career of thirty uninterrupted seasons.

*Richard Crooks rose from oratorio
to sing such persuasive
roles as Romeo in the 1937
revival of Gounod's opera.*

*Lily Pons made her debut as
Lucia, always one of her most
popular roles, in which her virtuosity
was seen from the first.*

A notable performance of *Tristan* on January 16 introduced two distinguished Wagnerian artists, Frida Leider and Maria Olszewska, playing opposite Lauritz Melchior and bringing the record of Wagner's passionate tragedy to the hundredth performance under Gatti's management.

The operatic year was further reduced to the shortest period in the history of the opera house in 1933-34, when a fourteen-week season was opened on December 26 with *Peter Ibbetson,* sung by its usual popular cast.

Several impressive Metropolitan careers were soon started in a variety of works. On December 27 the popular Austrian bass, Emanuel List, made his first appearance as the Landgraf Hermann in *Tannhauser.* On the twenty-ninth Irra Petina quietly started her long list of Metropolitan characterizations as a Valkyrie. The day before the lyric Italian tenor, Nino Martini, sang his first Duke in a *Rigoletto* matinee, while that same evening, Virgilio Lazzari appeared as Don Pedro in *l'Africana.*

New intensity was given to the role of Sieglinde in the January 11 *Walküre* by Lotte Lehmann, who soon added her glowing Elisabeth and engaging Eva.

Another infrequent but welcome visitor to the Metropolitan stage graced it for the first time on February 2 in the person of John Charles Thomas, who sang his first Germont at a benefit matinee.

While the season boasted only two novelties, Howard Hanson's *Merry Mount,* which was introduced by Serafin on February 10 with Johnson and Tibbett in the leading roles and Donizetti's *Linda di Chamounix,* which Lily Pons sang under the same baton on March 1, the revival of Strauss' *Salome* amounted to the introduction of a new work. Artur Bodanzky conducted the first performance on January 13 with Göta Ljungberg in the title role and Schorr as Jochanaan, while rich atmospheric settings were provided by Donald Oenslager.

The spring tour, which had been reduced in 1933 to three performances in Baltimore, now included Boston, for the first time in sixteen years.

In spite of the continued support of the Juilliard Foundation and the commercial sponsorship of the broadcasts, the Metropolitan again found itself hard put to it to meet rising expenses and the waning resources of its subscription public. On March 11 a "Surprise Party" was given to benefit the management, with many of the artists cast in unaccustomed and absurd roles. On April 14 a program of operatic excerpts was offered to secure additional revenue, and on the 27th a second opera ball completed the necessary fund with difficulty.

Gatti-Casazza's final season, 1934-35, was once more inaugurated by *Aïda* on Saturday, December 22, since it was decided to waive the usual Monday night precedent in view of its falling on Christmas Eve.

Faced by the lack of a soprano whose repertory included the heavier Wagnerian roles, the discouraged General Manager was soon to discover a gold mine in Kirsten Flagstad. Her presence, first hailed as Sieglinde on February 2, opened a new and glorious vista in the popularity of Wagner.

Kirsten Flagstad, whose imaginative insight animated the young Walküre *Brünnhilde in her third Metropolitan appearance.*

On February 6, the little-known Norwegian soprano was heard in her first Metropolitan Isolde, on the fifteenth, in her first *Walküre* Brünnhilde on any stage, her first *Götterdämmerung* Brünnhilde on the twenty-eighth and the first Kundry of her career in a post-season *Parsifal* on April 17. During these last eight weeks of the season she had also sung Elisabeth and Elsa, adding to a list of roles which, in the words of Lawrence Gilman, were "constantly enriched in beauty and significance from the seemingly inexhaustible store of her inspired sympathy and comprehension."

In other respects the Metropolitan pursued its straightened way with a number of revivals which seem surprising in view of the still serious influence of the depression. On February 23, *Don Pasquale* was restored to the repertory for Lucrezia Bori. On January 4, *Rosenkavalier* returned after a five-year absence, now renewed in its pathetic and comic appeal by the presence of Lotte Lehmann and Emanuel List. A single American novelty, Seymour's one-act opera, *In the Pasha's Garden,* served to introduce a new American soprano, the handsome Pennsylvanian, Helen Jepson, who was joined by Jagel and Tibbett.

On the March 19 an operatic gala was offered for the retiring General Manager, which also served to raise a substantial fund toward future administrative expenses. In his twenty-seven years at the Metropolitan helm, Giulio Gatti-Casazza had been lavish to present new works, new singers, new roles for established artists. It is characteristic that his last public gesture was to turn over the proceeds of his benefit to the "noble house" he had served so faithfully.

61

Opera Broadens National Scope
Under Edward Johnson

WHEN EDWARD JOHNSON was appointed General Manager of the Metropolitan Opera Association on May 15, 1935, the post was shadowed by the untimely death of Herbert Witherspoon, who on May 10 collapsed from a heart attack after six arduous weeks preparing to fill the position left vacant by Gatti.

The effects of the depression were not yet over. A handful of artists were all that had been definitely secured for the following year. The new General Manager had only his long experience as a leading figure in operetta and grand opera to draw on in his present predicament.

On the other side of the ledger stood a variety of assets. Kirsten Flagstad had promised to return to the opera house. Edward Ziegler, who since the season of 1932-33 had served as Assistant General Manager, provided a store of wisdom from his long association with Gatti. An opera management committee, consisting of John Erskine, chairman, Miss Bori, Cornelius N. Bliss and Allen Wardwell was formed on May 24 to aid the new management. Mrs. August Belmont, the first woman member of the Metropolitan Board, was at hand to plan and build up an organization of laymen, known as The Metropolitan Opera Guild, whose formation was announced on August 22. Johnson himself was an incorrigible optimist, blessed with a warm-hearted and magnetic personality.

The inaugural season of the new era opened on December 16, 1935 with *La Traviata*. Lucrezi Bori sang the title role in exquisite new Paris costumes for what proved to be the last time at the Metropolitan. Crooks and Tibbett played their accustomed parts. A new Flora, the Cleveland soprano Thelma Votipka, began her record-breaking list of secondary roles. New settings by Jonel Jorgulesco made a chic background for the American Ballet, which now assembled at the opera house under the direction of George Balanchine.

After repeating her popular Mimi, Mignon and Manon, Miss Bori reappeared on January 17 opposite Nino Martini as the heroine of Puccini's *La Rondine*, a role which she had created eight years before. A formal concert on the March 29 brought reminiscences of Sembrich's last appearance, as the beloved soprano sang her final Saint Sulpice scene and was decked by the directors in a beautiful diamond ornament of the Empress Eugenie.

Although no new operas were offered by Mr. Johnson in his first season, he presented no less than fifteen new singers, of whom nine were native Americans. Among the most outstanding was the Australian dramatic soprano, Marjorie Lawrence, who made an effective debut as Brünnhilde in *Die Walküre* on the second night of the season and later won the plaudits of the public by leaping on her steed Grane at the close of the January 11 *Götterdämmerung*.

Charles Kullman, a gifted tenor from New Haven who had deepened his operatic experience in Berlin, sang his first Faust on December 19.

The *Aïda* cast of December 20 included an outstanding Amneris, the Swedish mezzo soprano Gertrud Wettergren and on the March 2 performance the velvet-voiced contralto, Bruna Castagna, while Dusolina Giannini, a talented American of Italian parentage, sang the title role on February 12.

The *Lohengrin* of December 21 was especially praised for its stalwart Herald, the New England baritone Julius Huehn, who soon became a backbone of the Wagnerian repertory. Another valuable contributor to this field was the Belgian tenor, René Maison, who made his Metropolitan debut on February 2 as Walther in *Die Meistersinger*.

A new coloratura from Colorado, Josephine Antoine, made her debut in the January 4 *Mignon* as Philine.

For Flagstad admirers there was a revival of Beethoven's *Fidelio* on March 7 under Bodanzky's baton, with Maison singing Florestan.

Almost equal space was devoted by the press to Rosa Ponselle's first Carmen on December 27, which proved a brooding yet passionate interpretation.

In January Mr. Johnson initiated another precedent in the revival of *Gianni Schicchi* with an English text, the first of a dozen experiments in the vernacular. The production, featuring Lawrence Tibbett, was conducted by Gennaro Papi.

After the brief tour to Boston, Rochester and Baltimore that followed the fourteen weeks of opera in New York, the Metropolitan embarked on the first of two spring seasons at popular prices, in which young American singers were featured and many performances were given in English.

Of the thirteen debuts which occurred during May, 1936, nine disclosed American talent. On the thirteenth of the month three young singers appeared in *Rigoletto* at the threshold of active operatic careers: Norman Cordon sang Monterone; John Gurney, Sparafucile and Anna Kaskas, Maddalena.

Miss Kaskas shared with the English tenor, Arthur Carron, who made his Metropolitan debut in a spring season *Pagliacci* as Canio, the honor of being the first to win the Metropolitan Opera Auditions of the Air, which closed its first season, under the artistic direction of Wilfred Pelletier, the previous March. Maxine Stellman, who was to enter the Auditions the following February, was another May debutante, together with Lucielle Browning and others.

Perhaps the most provocative novelty of the month was a production of *Orfeo*, acted in pantomime by the American Ballet with modernistic choreography and settings by Balanchine and the painter Tchelitchev. More popular with the general public was an English revival of *The Bartered Bride*, with Muriel Dickson, formerly a leading soprano in the D'Oyly Carte Company, in the title role and with the gifted comedian George Rasely as Wenzel.

From the performance of Mr. Johnson's second season, when *Die Walküre* was directed by Artur Bodanzky on December 21, 1936, an improvement in the quality of the orchestral tone was noted. Honors were shared with Flagstad and Melchior by the Swedish contralto, Kerstin Thorborg.

During the first week a new conductor, Maurice de Abravanel, led his first *Samson et Dalila* on December 26, while a new vitality was infused into the production by a new stage director, Herbert Graf.

Flagstad brought an authentic Norwegian quality to the role of Senta in *The Flying Dutchman* on January 7 and sang eight Isoldes during the winter. In the January 22 *Siegfried* she completed her cycle of Brünnhildes.

For Lily Pons there was a revival of *Coq d'Or* on February 4, with the diminutive French soprano skillfully dancing as well as singing the role of the queen, opposite Ezio Pinza, and Doris Doe enacting Amelfa, the Nurse.

Two days later a new dramatic soprano, Gina Cigna, made her bow as Aïda, and on February 13 the tiny Brazilian soprano, Bidu Sayao, first brought her

Marjorie Lawrence as the Walküre *Brünnhilde. She sang the first lines in French, fresh from the Paris stage.*

Bidu Sayao introduced her touching Violetta to the Metropolitan public in March, 1937, her first N.Y. season.

Kerstin Thorborg as Kundry in Parsifal, a role she first sang at the Metropolitan in 1942.

64

ingratiating presence to the role of Manon. Four days after this John Brownlee, the popular Australian baritone, inaugurated a fine career with Rigoletto.

Mr. Johnson continued his experiments of opera in English with a revival of Cimarosa's *Clandestine Marriage;* further repetitions of *The Bartered Bride,* both with Muriel Dickson, and finally the premiere on February 4 of a new American work, Richard Hageman's *Caponsacchi,* which gave visual and musical form to Browning's poem, *The Ring and the Book.* Helen Jepson, Lawrence Tibbett and Mario Chamlee sang the leading roles with Norman Cordon as the Pope.

Other useful additions to the company this season were Irene Jessner, who sang Hänsel first on Christmas Eve and Karl Laufkötter, *Tristan* Shepherd.

Cleveland was once more added by the Metropolitan Company to its spring tour in 1937 and once more the younger artists gathered in New York in May for a brief season at popular prices, now under Lee Pattison.

The news event of the month was the world premiere of Walter Damrosch's *Man Without a Country* on May 12. The most enduring effect of this production on the history of the Metropolitan, however, was the introduction of the St. Louis soprano, Helen Traubel, who returned three years later as a Wagnerian star.

Louis D'Angelo's Kezal, the marriage broker, and Mario Chamlee's Jenik helped to make the English version of The Bartered Bride *a hit in May, 1936.*

Jussi Bjoerling did not sing the Rigoletto Duke *until New Year's Day, 1940, after Rodolfo and Manrico.*

Le Coq D'Or, *revived at the Opera House in 1937 in French, was the first occasion in New York when singers both mimed and sang their roles. Here Lily Pons as the Princess appears before Ezio Pinza, King Dodon.*

In the third act of Otello, *revived in December, 1937, Martinelli as the Moor and Tibbett as Iago are warned by the Herald, Wilfred Engelman. Donald Oenslager's new settings suggested the brilliance of Cyprus.*

The death of Simon Boccanegra in the opera revived for Tibbett, Caniglia, Pinza and Martinelli under Panizza's baton in January, 1939. On this occasion Leonard Warren made his debut as Paolo, later singing the lead.

An English version of Henri Rabaud's *Marouf* was conducted by Wilfred Pelletier on May 21 with Chamlee in the title role.

The popularity of *Tristan und Isolde,* as portrayed by Melchior and Flagstad, which warranted nine presentations at the Opera House during the season of 1937-38, was also attested in its choice for the opening night on November 29. Once more the Metropolitan announced a sixteen-week season. The successful debut of Erich Leinsdorf on the podium at the *Walküre* of January 21 suggested that even the absence of Bodanzky could not impair Wagnerian standards.

It is not only by Wagner, however, that Johnson's third season is remembered. All three of the leading dramas of Richard Strauss were presented this year, *Der Rosenkavalier* and *Elektra* under Bodanzky's baton, *Salome* led by Ettore Panizza. Kerstin Thorborg first sang the title role of the comedy on December 1, with Lotte Lehmann as the incomparable Marschallin. She reappeared as Klytemnestra on January 7, when Rose Pauly first officiated as the Greek heroine with Jessner, Schorr and Althouse. Marjorie Lawrence was the season's Salome.

It was the Italian repertory which served to present most of the new artists of the season. Of those who took the most prominent place in future years were Zinka Milanov, the warm-voiced Yugoslavian soprano who made her debut as Leonora in the *Trovatore* of December 17 and was especially praised for her mellifluous pianissimos, and Nicola Moscona, the powerful Greek basso, who sang his first Ramfis on the thirteenth of the month.

Of briefer appearance in the roster were three tenors: the Pole, Jan Kiepura, who sang his first electric Rodolfo on February 10, the Italian Bruno Landi, who first appeared as the *Rigoletto* Duke on January 12 and Carl Hartmann, a convincing Siegfried.

Another novelty in the English language was Gian-Carlo Menotti's *Amelia Goes to the Ball,* which was offered on March 3 with Donald Oenslager's settings.

This talented designer was also responsible for the most important revival of the season, Verdi's *Otello,* which was offered on December 22 with Martinelli, Rethberg and Tibbett in the leading roles.

In recognition of *Otello's* success, it was chosen to open the season of 1938-39 with a new Italian soprano, Maria Caniglia, singing Desdemona on November 21.

This turned out to be something of a Verdi year with revivals of *Falstaff* on December 16 and *Simon Boccanegra* on January 13 with Tibbett in both title roles, as well as the familiar *Trovatores, Traviatas, Rigolettos* and *Aïdas.*

The Metropolitan once more presented its own ballet, now under the imaginative direction of Boris Romanoff. The new ballet master was particularly happy in his choreography for *Orfeo,* a revival featuring Kerstin Thorborg.

Among the most distinguished European newcomers of the year were Jussi Bjoerling, the young Swedish tenor, who sang his first Rodolfo on November 24; Herbert Janssen, the German baritone whose lyric gifts were well displayed in his first Wolfram on January 28 and the Italian tenor Alessio De Paolis, who made a

Gladys Swarthout as Carmen, a role to which the handsome mezzo-soprano rose in the Spring of 1940.

Jarmila Novotna as Octavian, a part which the soprano anticipated with Mimi, Cherubino and Smetana's Marie.

When Ezio Pinza first sang Boris Godunoff at the Metropolitan in 1939 new majesty crowned the Czar.

keen impression for his finely etched characterizations from his first Cassio on December 3. Beniamino Gigli briefly returned to sing Radames on January 23.

"One of the major accomplishments in Johnson's regime," according to the historian, Irving Kolodin, was the revival of *Boris Godunoff* on March 7, with Ezio Pinza singing the title role and Leonard Warren as Rangoni, the Jesuit.

This young New York baritone had made his operatic debut on January 13 in *Simon Boccanegra*, having won his Metropolitan contract through the Metropolitan Auditions of the Air the previous season. Soon he took stellar roles.

Another discovery of the auditions was the handsome and gifted New York mezzo soprano, Risë Stevens. Having withdrawn from the contest to secure further stage experience in Europe. Miss Stevens now returned to make her Metropolitan debut in Philadelphia as Octavian opposite Marita Farell's personable Sophie on November 22 and in New York as Mignon on December 17.

Two other American prima donnas were featured in the two French revivals of 1938-39: Grace Moore in Charpentier's *Louise* on January 28 — a reminder of the motion picture which she had recently made under the composer's direction — and Helen Jepson in Massenet's *Thaïs* on February 10.

The season was also signalized by the advancement of Earle R. Lewis, who had been a member of the staff since the arrival of Gatti-Casazza, to the position of Assistant General Manager.

The company this year reached as far as Dallas and New Orleans in its spring tour and then returned for a series of nine performances of the Wagner music dramas in May, a gesture of cooperation with the World's Fair management.

The success of *Simon Boccanegra* earned for Verdi's revised masterpiece the honor of opening the season of 1939-40 on November 27, when Lawrence Tibbett was heard with Rethberg, Martinelli and Pinza.

The death of Arthur Bodanzky the following day was a heavy blow to the Wagnerian wing, but young Erich Leinsdorf bravely undertook the bulk of his responsibilities. New sources of strength for this field were also at hand in the return of Helen Traubel, who sang her first Metropolitan Sieglinde on December 28 and Alexander Kipnis, whose Gurnemanz added to the *Parsifal* of January 5.

Giuseppe Sturani, who had presided as Musical Secretary after his retirement as a Metropolitan conductor, also died this season, but was replaced by Frank St. Leger, who acted in a dual capacity at desk and podium.

The Italian repertory flourished with new vitality because of two radiant additions to the soprano roster. On January 5 the beautiful Czech, Jarmila Novotna, sang her first Mimi and promptly won the hearts of the public. On February 9 Licia Albanese, a young lyric soprano from Bari, sang her first Butterfly, a sensitive characterization which she had inherited through her teacher, Baldassare-Tedeschi, from the original Cio-Cio-San, Rosina Storchio.

February also saw a new des Grieux, the accomplished Canadian tenor, Raoul Jobin, who made his debut on February 19, while on the seventh of the month

Albanese's debut as Butterfly called forth tears and cheers from the public. Here she is seen in the poignant second act telling Consul Sharpless, played by John Brownlee, of her romance.

the veteran baritone, Giuseppe De Luca, returned from Rome to bring down the house with his well-loved characterization of Germont.

The two winners of the Auditions of the Air this season, Annamary Dickey and Mack Harrell, were introduced in *Orfeo* and *Tannhäuser* respectively, where one sang the Happy Shade, the other Biterolf.

A brilliant new production embellished the revival of *Le Nozze di Figaro*, which was restored to the repertory for the first time in twenty years at a gala performance on February 20. New scenery was designed for the occasion by Jonel Jorgulesco; dashing new costumes were prepared by Ladislas Czettel, while an all-star cast, led by Pinza in the title role under Panizza's baton, brought new smoothness, vivacity and polish to the ensemble: a distinctive contribution.

A crisis in Metropolitan history was reached this year when it became necessary for the Metropolitan Opera Association to purchase the theatre from the Metropolitan Opera and Real Estate Company which had held title since 1893. On January 27 a nation-wide drive to raise $1,000,000 was announced over the air. By the time that the company set forth on the spring tour, to which Atlanta was now added, the goal was reached. From henceforth the producing company was the possessor of its own opera house.

The new gold curtain which had been made possible by the 1940 campaign for funds rose on December 2, the opening night of the 1940-41 season, to display a new production. The opera was *Un Ballo in Maschera*, Verdi's much-censored work which was now transplanted, thanks to the imagination of the Russian artist Dobujinsky, to the original Swedish locale of the play from which it was

René Maison and Marjorie Lawrence enact the classical story of Admetus and Alcestis at the Metropolitan premiere of Gluck's rarely given work under the baton of Ettore Panizza in 1941.

derived. Appropriately enough two Swedes sang leading roles, Jussi Bjoerling and Kerstin Thorborg, while Zinka Milanov impersonated the passionate heroine, and a new Hungarian baritone, Alexander Sved, sang Renato's popular *Eri Tu*.

The following night the inimitable Roman basso buffo, Salvatore Baccaloni, made his debut with the company as Bartolo, in a Philadelphia performance of *Le Nozze di Figaro* which he repeated within the week in New York. On December 21 *Don Pasquale* was revived at the Opera House, providing a more impressive part for the popular comedian.

A revival of Donizetti's *La Fille du Régiment*, in which Lily Pons vivaciously impersonated the winsome heroine in the story-book setting of Jonel Jorgulesco, also kept the theatre in a ripple of laughter over Baccaloni's antics as Sulpice.

A lofty classical note was struck on January 24, 1941, in the premiere of Gluck's *Alceste*, assigned to Marjorie Lawrence, who later shared the title role with Rose Bampton, while René Maison made a regal Admetus. For this production new settings were designed by Richard Rychtarik.

Still a third new production was the work of Harry Horner, who devised practical and at the same time atmospheric settings for the revival of *Trovatore*.

One of the most eloquent delineations of Kirsten Flagstad was her Fidelio of February 14, when Bruno Walter made his debut as guest conductor, restoring the original spoken recitatives of Mahler's time and breathing new spiritual meaning into Beethoven's drama of the triumph of true love.

Other significant debuts of the season were the first appearance of Stella Roman in the New Year's Day *Aïda* and Francesco Valentino's first Ashton in *Lucia* on December 9.

On the first Saturday night of the season, December 7, Eleanor Steber, a young soprano from Wheeling, West Virginia, proved herself worthy to join Lotte Lehmann and Risë Stevens in the final trio of *Rosenkavalier,* the climax of her debut as Sophie.

In the opening week *Samson* on December 6, two American men sang modest roles. One was Arthur Kent, a promising baritone soon to be sidetracked from an operatic career by the call to arms. The other, Emery Darcy, turned out to be a *Heldentenor* in the making, whom Mr. Johnson was to watch carefully.

An event of historic interest was Italo Montemezzi's first appearance on the podium to conduct his own *L'Amore dei tre re* with Grace Moore and Charles Kullman on February 7.

The widest tour taken by the Metropolitan Company in thirty years was saddened, this spring, by the announcement that Kirsten Flagstad was singing her last performance with her colleagues "until the war is over." A few weeks later news came that Marjorie Lawrence had been stricken by paralysis in Mexico.

Another severe loss had been sustained in the death of Paul D. Cravath, for thirty years a director of the operating company, and for nearly ten chairman and then president of its board. Yet his successor as president, George A. Sloan, was proving worthy of the post, a sturdy coadjutor to Mr. Bliss as chairman.

And for the first time since the names of six masters had been engraved on the proscenium: Gluck, Mozart, Beethoven, Gounod, Verdi and Wagner, the Metropolitan could boast of presenting operas by all six in a single season.

THE METROPOLITAN IN ANOTHER WORLD WAR 1941-45

The one hundred and fiftieth anniversary of the death of Mozart was often remembered during the season of 1941-42, which opened with a joyous performance of *Le Nozze di Figaro* under Ettore Panizza's baton. Ezio Pinza and Bidu Sayao once more impersonated the humble lovers; John Brownlee and Elisabeth Rethberg, the Count and Countess; Risë Stevens, Cherubino and Baccaloni, Bartolo.

Soon an English version of *The Magic Flute* by Thomas and Ruth Martin introduced the Metropolitan public to Mozart's fairy-land fantasy, which was presented on December 11 with fabulous settings by Richard Rychtarik. A new spiritual meaning invested the little *Singspiel,* thanks to Bruno Walter and Herbert Graf, while the gentle Paminas of Jarmila Novotna and later Nadine Conner and the ardent Tamino of Charles Kullman contributed to a human drama whose goal was set by Alexander Kipnis' majestic Sarastro. John Brownlee and Natalie Bodanya made merry as Papageno and Papagena.

A third Mozart opera, *Don Giovanni,* appropriately memorialized the actual day of the composer's death, December 5, when it was conducted by Bruno Walter with Pinza in the title role, one of the magnetic basso's happiest parts.

Another guest conductor added variety to the repertory this year in the witty presence of Sir Thomas Beecham. At his first appearance he introduced his own operatic version of Bach's cantata *Phoebus and Pan,* a lavish baroque production

For ten years, 1935-1945,
Lotte Lehmann enacted her
incomparable Marschallin.

Jan Peerce as Cavaradossi,
a New York tenor with an
art which suggested Italy.

Licia Albanese perfected
her Violetta at the Metropolitan: poignant, personal.

Margaret Harshaw's sumptuous
voice found an ideal
vehicle in Wagner's Ortrud.

The first American Isolde since Nordica,
Helen Traubel proved a worthy successor.

for which Rychtarik had designed elaborate costumes and a picturesque background. The little work was billed with Rimsky-Korsakoff's *Cop d'Or* on January 15 and was followed the next week by Sir Thomas' lively interpretation of *Carmen*, with new costumes by Mary Percy Schenck.

The Bizet heroine was played for the first time in this performance by the Belgian soprano Lily Djanel, who was applauded for her vivacious rendering.

Baccaloni found a new vehicle in Doctor Dulcamara in *L'Elisir d'Amore*, which was revived on November 28 with Bidu Sayao and Bruno Landi.

The Italian repertory also gained much from the arrival of Jan Peerce, an American tenor who was first heard as Alfredo in the November 29 *Traviata*, an otherwise tragic occasion, since Gennaro Papi, who had been assigned to conduct the performance, was found dead of a heart attack in his hotel, a few minutes before the curtain rose.

Kurt Baum modestly inaugurated a Metropolitan career of distinction as the Singer in the November 27 *Rosenkavalier*.

Deprived of the presence of Flagstad and Lawrence, and including no performance of *Tristan* for the first time in twenty years, the season still gained strength for Wagner, Astrid Varnay, an American dramatic soprano of Scandinavian birth and Hungarian parentage, made an exciting debut, replacing the indisposed Lotte Lehmann as Sieglinde in a broadcast *Walküre* on December 6. Six days later Miss Varnay substituted for Helen Traubel in her first Brünnhilde and repeated the favorable impression of her debut.

On February 20 Miss Varnay had the honor of creating a new heroine on the Metropolitan stage, one of the central figures of Gian-Carlo Menotti's philosophic yet moving drama, *The Island God*, which Panizza conducted with Jobin, Warren, Cordon and Carter in the other roles.

Lothar Wallerstein, who served as stage director, vitalized the Wagner performances this year and also proved valuable in giving stage training to some of the younger members of the company.

The young German tenor John Garris made an unpretentious debut as the First Knight in the February 27 *Parsifal*, which he followed with other highly musical interpretations. Gerhard Pechner as the Notary in *Der Rosenkavalier*

Johnson's revival of Le Nozze di Figaro *was acclaimed as a triumph of ensemble. The public also enjoyed its excellent theatre, especially the intricate by-play of the second act with Rethberg, Pinza, Sayao, DePaolis, Brownlee, Petina and Lazzari.*

74

and Osie Hawkins as Donner in *Rheingold* were also well received.

Meanwhile the ballet prospered under the new direction of Laurent Novikoff, a former partner of Anna Pavlowa and an authoritative ballet master.

Changes were also evident in the business offices of the Metropolitan Opera Association, from which Frank Garlichs had retired after forty-three years of service, to be replaced by Frederick P. Keppel Jr. as Comptroller.

The traditional good luck which Lily Pons attaches to the number thirteen befell her on November 23, 1942, when for the first time she was honored by opening the season — her thirteenth at the Metropolitan. *La Fille du Régiment* was gay with flags; the house sparkled with military and naval uniforms. Baccaloni and Petina roused laughter and Jobin added the necessary pathos.

Within the week Miss Pons reappeared in another Donizetti work, *Lucia di Lammermoor*, singing opposite Jan Peerce against a fresh romantic background designed by Richard Rychtarik, with magnificent new costumes.

Mr. Johnson's policy of dividing the repertory among a series of important conductors won new acclaim this year when the dynamic Czech, George Szell, led a stirring performance of *Salome* on December 9, with Lily Djanel. Soon Mr. Szell was heard in a revival of *Boris Godunoff*, in which Alexander Kipnis sang the haunted Czar for the first time on February 19.

Bruno Walter meanwhile evoked the religious values as well as the fateful melodrama from *La Forza del Destino,* which was presented for the first time in eight years on January 9, with Zinka Milanov, Kurt Baum and Lawrence Tibbett. Mr. Walter also undertook the Mozart performances this season.

Sir Thomas Beecham added *Louise* and *Faust* to his French assignments, while a new Italian conductor, Cesare Sodero, brought the fruits of his long practical experience in radio to the older Verdi operas. Erich Leinsdorf still presided over Wagner, and Paul Breisach and Wilfred Pelletier were also kept busy.

In spite of the war, three new European artists were added to the roster this season: the French tenor Jacques Gérard, who sang his first Gerald in the December 2 *Lakmé;* a young Viennese mezzo soprano, Hertha Glaz, who first appeared as Amneris on Christmas night, and a versatile Hungarian bass, Lorenzo Alvary.

Nicola Moscona, seen here as Sarastro in the brotherhood ceremonial of The Magic Flute, *shared this role with Kipnis and Pinza in the English revival of Mozart's fantasy in 1941 under Bruno Walter's direction. Settings by Rychtarik.*

75

When Puccini's amusing Gianni Schicchi *was revived in 1944 the title role was sung by Salvatore Baccaloni. Here we see him surrounded by his grasping accomplices, reading from left to right:..*

The first *Götterdämmerung* on November 25 was praised for its trio of Norns, who included one of the 1942 prize winners of the air, Margaret Harshaw and a young dramatic soprano from New Jersey, Doris Doree.

Another talented alumna of the Auditions, Frances Greer, first appeared as Musetta on November 30, while still a third, the tenor Elwood Gary, opened a brief engagement at the Opera House in *Rosenkavalier*.

James Melton, a lyric tenor from Georgia who had already won a following on the radio, made his debut as Tamino in *The Magic Flute* on December 7, when Lillian Raymondi, a diminutive soprano from Scranton, Pa., a protegee of Frances Alda, repeated the favorable impression of her debut as Papagena.

The withdrawal of two veteran members of the Wagnerian wing deprived the Metropolitan of Elisabeth Rethberg and Friedrich Schorr this year, although the Austrian baritone remained to sing a final Wanderer on February 23.

Wagner prospered nevertheless when Helen Traubel sang her first magnificent Isolde on December 4 and when Marjorie Lawrence, although still forced to sing in a recumbent position, was given an ovation for her Venus on January 22.

Giacomo Spadoni, who hitherto had acted as assistant conductor, was made chorus master this year, sharing his duties with Konrad Neuger.

The choice of *Boris Godunoff* to open the Diamond Jubilee Season of 1943-44

Frances Greer, Virgilio Lazzari, Thelma Votipka, Gerhard Pechner, Alessio De Paolis, and right of Mr. Baccaloni: Nino Martini, George Cehanovsky, Anna Kaskas, assembled by Cesare Sodero.

on November 22 struck the editorial writers of the New York *Times* as a "particularly felicitous" gesture of good will to Russia, whose military successes were filling the front pages.

Crowded houses continued to be the rule at the Metropolitan throughout the season. With this warm approval of the public the repertory continued to retain its international standard, while no offense was taken at the sound of enemy tongues. The prejudices of a quarter century before were forgotten.

Though shadowed by the announcement of Karin Branzell's approaching temporary retirement, the Wagnerian performances continued their high quality. They were further enriched by Marjorie Lawrence's first Isolde in New York when, on March 14, she gave a heroic and supremely effective performance, although remaining seated on the stage.

The production of *Les Contes D'Hoffmann*, newly decorated by Joseph Novak and staged by Herbert Graf, provided Sir Thomas Beecham with a sympathetic vehicle for his sparkling baton on December 10. The role of Olympia the doll fitted the neat coloratura of eighteen-year-old Patrice Munsel, a prizewinner of the 1943 Auditions of the Air, who had made her debut as Philine in *Mignon*, opposite Donald Dame's stylish Laerte, the week before.

Another newcomer of the Offenbach cast was the French baritone, Martial Singher, who was later featured in *Pelléas et Mélisande*, opposite Bidu Sayao, under the baton of the Russian maestro, Emil Cooper.

Sir Thomas inspired an almost all-American cast for the revival of Verdi's *Falstaff* in English on January 14, lending his own skill to the translation and fusing a smooth ensemble, led by Lawrence Tibbett and Eleanor Steber. Later Leonard Warren reached a new peak in his career by appearing as the fat knight.

Other newcomers of the season were Thelma Altman, a young mezzo soprano who sang the Czarevich on opening night, the New Jersey baritone John Baker and the Kentucky mezzo soprano Christine Johnson — both winners of the Auditions of the Air; Christina Carroll, a new Musetta of Rumanian birth; Ella Flesch, a dramatic soprano from Budapest, who brought Richard Strauss' personal directions to her first Salome; Frederick Lechner, a competent baritone from Stettin, Jennie Tourel, a talented Carmen and Mignon and Audrey Bowman, an English soprano who sang the Queen of the Night with rare dramatic fervor.

The Diamond Jubilee Season proved successful both in its box office receipts and in the testimony of confidence indicated in the nationwide drive to raise $300,000. Thanks to the loyal public, this goal was surpassed by $50,000.

An emphasis on musical theatre characterized the tenth season of Edward Johnson's regime, 1944-45, and was soon recognized by the press.

War-time restrictions still prevented the importation of European artists but did not diminish the management's zeal. "We are fighting to preserve our cultural as well as our political institutions," reiterated Mr. Johnson, announcing the engagement of fifteen young American singers.

The Metropolitan Opera Auditions of the Air introduced four new members to the roster: Morton Bowe, William Hargrave, Regina Resnik and Hugh Thompson. Of these Miss Resnik was commended for her "confidence and authority" at her unheralded debut in *Trovatore* and soon found herself promoted to the title role of *Fidelio* in an English revival with Bruno Walter at the podium on March 17. The same evening Kenneth Schon made his debut at Pizarro, hailed for his "dignity and dramatic power."

Another English experiment was the revival of *The Golden Cockerel* on March 1 under Emil Cooper, who had conducted the world premiere in 1909. In spite of the skill of the conductor, the charms of Patrice Munsel as the Princess and the comic sense of Norman Cordon as the King, the work did not endure.

Among the high spots of the season were the revival of *Die Meistersinger* on January 12, with Eleanor Steber, Kerstin Thorborg, Charles Kullman and Herbert Janssen singing under George Szell's baton and the production of *La Gioconda* on January 25, when Richard Tucker made a noteworthy debut as Enzo..

Another newcomer, Blanche Thebom of Ohio, presented an outstanding contribution to the Wagnerian wing as Brangaene and Fricka.

On February 23, Lotte Lehmann interpreted her last unforgettable Marschallin. A rare feat took place on March 14: Jennie Tourel's Rosina in the original version planned by Rossini for a mezzo soprano.

Patrice Munsel, youngest singer at the Metropolitan, was cast as Rosina in her second season.

Zinka Milanov sang her first Norma in the Opera House in 1943, a passionate interpretation.

Risë Stevens conceives Carmen as fatalistic and passive but her dances are full of vitality.

Leonard Warren's Rigoletto is esteemed as a convincing and moving interpretation by a notable American.

Dorothy Kirsten's Marguerite was charming to eye and ear when first seen and heard in March, 1947.

The 1945 revival of Die Meistersinger under George Szell featured Charles Kullman as Walther.
His Prize Song, as seen
here with John Garris as David
at the left, was the climax of
the third act. Janssen was the
Sachs, Eleanor Steber the Eva.

Josef Urban's settings for
Roméo et Juliette still evoke a
romantic mood. Bidu Sayao, seen
here in the last act, shared
the role with Patrice Munsel in
the revival of 1946 under Emil
Cooper with Jussi Bjoerling, Jobin
and Kullman as the Roméo.

The finale of Humperdinck's Hänsel
and Gretel as revived in December,
1946 under Guild auspices.
Fritz Stiedry conducted, with
Brownlee, Conner, Stevens and
Turner in the leading roles seen in
the center of the picture. Recordings preserve the joy of the music.

The first opening night performance to be broadcast from the Metropolitan was the *Lohengrin* of November 26, 1945, with a new conductor, Fritz Busch, and a new Swedish tenor, Torsten Ralf.

Even before opening night a preview of *Roméo et Juliette* had been offered by the Opera Guild for the Production Fund, with Munsel, Jobin and Singher.

Another revival of the season was a double bill, Puccini's *Il Tabarro* and Donizetti's *Don Pasquale,* presented on January 5 with Albanese, Jagel and Tibbett in the former; Sayao, Martini, Brownlee and Baccaloni in the latter.

First post-war importations from Europe included Joel Berglund, whose "pliant, colorful and resonant voice" was first heard as Hans Sachs on January 9; Giacomo Vaghi, who was applauded as Colline, Alvise and Basilio and Ramon Vinay, who sang his first Don José on Washington's Birthday.

Of the American newcomers, Dorothy Kirsten was instantly recognized as a stellar attraction from her first Mimi on December 1 and was soon offered Juliette and Violetta. Florence Quartararo was introduced as Micaela and later added Pamina. The three auditionists of the air, Robert Merrill, Pierrette Alarie and Thomas Hayward made helpful contributions, especially Mr. Merrill, whose Germont on December 15 was followed by an effective Ashton and Toreador.

Meanwhile Kurt Adler was elevated to the rank of chorus master, Dino Yannopoulos started his New York career as stage director with *Tabarro* and the new ballet master, Edward Caton, proved also an excellent mime.

The return of Jussi Bjoerling, absent during the war years, gave a new impetus to *Bohème* and *Ballo in Maschera*. Risë Stevens sang her first Carmen with the company and Grace Moore a final *Tosca* before her untimely death.

The Metropolitan administration was shadowed by the retirement of Edward Ziegler as Assistant General Manager but stimulated by the election of George A. Sloan, who succeeded Mr. Bliss as Chairman of the Board, a vacancy almost impossible to fill. The able lawyer, Charles M. Spofford, was made president.

Through the co-operation of the Texas Company, sponsors of the broadcasts, the Opera Guild distributed a ballot through the radio audience for the choice of six operas to be broadcast the following season. *Aïda, Carmen, Traviata* and *Tristan* were voted most popular among the standard operas; *Hansel and Gretel, Boris Godunoff* and *Der Rosenkavalier* led the less familiar list.

In addition to these operas, all of which were broadcast during the season of 1946-47, the Metropolitan offered two novelties this year in English. One of these was short-lived, a version of the Samson story by Bernard Rogers to a text of Norman Corwin entitled *The Warrior,* whose production on January 12 was made possible by the Alice J. Ditson award of Columbia University. In spite of the sturdy efforts of Regina Resnik and Mack Harrell under the baton of Max Rudolf, the work did not catch public fancy, though sharing the bill with *Hansel and Gretel*. Humperdinck's fairy opera was so happily cast with Risë Stevens and Nadine Conner in the title roles that it was chosen as the first work to be recorded from the Metropolitan stage by Columbia in June.

Although the other Metropolitan novelty, Mozart's *Abduction from the Seraglio,* was entrusted to Eleanor Steber, Charles Kullman, Deszo Ernster and Pierrette Alarie under Cooper's direction on November 29 and colorfully set by Donald Oenslager, the work was withdrawn after five performances.

Debuts of interest were Set Svanholm's vigorous Siegfried on November 15 under Fritz Stiedry's expert baton and Ferruccio Tagliavini's vociferous reception as Rodolfo on January 10. Daniza Ilitsch gave promise in her first Desdemona. Jerome Hines and Leslie Chabay offered assurance of value.

An accident which befell Melchior in *Die Walküre,* when the tenor broke his toe, tripping on crumbling scenery, called public attention to the need of new sets for the *Ring of the Nibelung,* which had not been produced in its entirety since 1945. The Opera Guild took the initiative for this enterprise and by the following spring announced that a total of $165,000 had been reached.

Edward Johnson was elected to the Association Board this season, which was also significant for the most extensive tour in the organization's history, a total of sixty-seven performances in fifteen cities.

1947-48 set a new record, 137 performances of twenty-nine operas in New York, the fullest season of the Johnson regime.

Lee Simonson's new settings for the *Ring* attracted a wide variety of praise and blame when two cycles were offered, the first, under Guild auspices in January featuring Traubel and Melchior with Stiedry as conductor.

Novelty of the season, Benjamin Britten's *Peter Grimes,* introduced on February 12 by Emil Cooper with Jagel and Resnik sharing the leads with Brian Sullivan and Polyna Stoska, proved palatable to the sophisticated. Four performances

"Youthful in action as well as in song," the Times *hailed Set Svanholm at his debut as Siegfried.*

Richard Tucker as the Rigoletto *Duke, a role which fulfilled the promise of his 1945 debut as Enzo.*

Ferruccio Tagliavini's Edgardo brought down the house, just as his first Rodolfo had done.

in New York were followed by two on tour.

From Charpentier, aging composer of *Louise*, Dorothy Kirsten brought a vivid interpretation to the December 12 revival. Cloe Elmo made a distinct impression in her debut as Azucena on November 19. Giuseppe Valdengo was an effective Tonio in *Pagliacci*. Young Giuseppe Di Stefano was warmly received as the Duke in *Rigoletto* on February 25. A new conductor, Giuseppe Antonicelli, was entrusted with the revival of *Ballo in Maschera* and the *Tosca* in which Elen Dosia and later Pia Tassinari were heard. Max Lorenz returned after fourteen years' absence to sing Tristan. The spring tour completed a new record for Johnson: 71 performances in seventeen cities.

Astrid Varnay as Ortrud, a role the versatile soprano varies with Elsa in Lohengrin, *two of her many fine Wagnerian parts.*

Eleanor Steber waited for nine years to sing the Rosenkavalier *Marschallin after her debut·Sophie.*

Ljuba Welitch was the sensation of 1949 with the clarion tones of her Salome and the fervor which Strauss loved.

Paul Schoeffler has many variations for Scarpia, from the lusty policeman to the smooth baron.

83

The *Otello* which opened the 1948-49 season with Albanese, Vinay and Warren, Fritz Busch conducting, was delayed until November 29 by the cancellation of the season on August 4. This was not rescinded until August 23, when an agreement was reached with the unions. But when the curtain rose, the performance was seen by an audience in the millions. Thanks to the American Broadcasting Company and the sponsoring Texas Company, *Otello* was telecast.

Outstanding among the season's revivals was the double bill of *Gianni Schicchi* and *Salome* on February 4. Led by Fritz Reiner, Ljuba Welitch made an unforgettable impression and the work was played five times in six weeks.

Lawrence Tibbett celebrated his twenty-fifth anniversary, after singing Balstrode in *Peter Grimes;* Papa Senz, the wigmaker, gave a party on his eightieth birthday. Mr. Johnson was decorated by Brazil, Italy, and Sweden.

The revival of the Auditions of the Air brought four young singers to the Company, of whom Frank Guarrera showed distinctive promise. Italo Tajo and Lubomir Vichegonov arrived from Europe: two important and talented basses.

In February the Association instituted a campaign with Opera Guild collaboration to guarantee the following season, assure new productions for Mr. Johnson's final year and provide engineering and architectural studies on which permanent maintenance and high production standards might be based.

Edward Johnson's fifteenth and last season as General Manager was inaugurated on November 21, 1949, with *Der Rosenkavalier.* This served as a memorial to Richard Strauss, recently deceased; a debut vehicle for Erna Berger and Peter Klein and an opportunity for Eleanor Steber to sing her first Marschallin, opposite Risë Stevens' popular Octavian. Again the work was telecast.

First of the new productions made possible by the Fund raised the previous year was *Manon Lescaut,* a revival on November 23 with settings by Krehan-Crayon. Kirsten, Bjoerling, Valdengo and Baccaloni sang leading roles.

A Metropolitan novelty was Moussorgsky's *Khovanchina,* presented in English on February 16 with Tibbett, Kullman, Hines, Stevens, etc. and authentic settings by Mstislav Dobujinsky. Emil Cooper, who conducted, edited the score.

Ferdinand Frantz and Paul Schoeffler added distinction to the list of baritones, Eugene Conley to the tenors, Jonel Perlea to the podium.

A gala testimonial was offered to the retiring General Manager on February 28 when Welitch sang her first local Tosca. A second performance provided for the overflow in April, raising the new Johnson Reserve Fund to $52,000.

The resignation of Earle R. Lewis and Frank St. Leger focused the interest and affection of the public and many gifts were lavished on the triumvirate.

The 1,800 performances of 72 operas credited to the administration of Edward Johnson included a variety of achievements. Mozart became a box-office attraction. Strauss came into his own. Wagner enjoyed magnificent ensemble.

Out of a lean exchequer, burdened with high production costs, Mr. Johnson produced nourishing fare. Out of a difficult and harassed era he brought consolation to a vast new public. Out of necessity itself he created virtue.

The finale of Das Rheingold *in Lee Simonson's new setting with Schon, Thorborg, Berglund, Darcy, Hines, Stoska and Szekely as the gods assembled under Fritz Stiedry's baton in the revival of January, 1948, sponsored by the Opera Guild.*

A scene from Benjamin Britten's Peter Grimes *in which the school teacher, Ellen Orford pleads with the people of the Borough for understanding of the unhappy fisherman. The choruses of the work were an eloquent and moving feature.*

Oriental dancers entertain the proud Prince Khovansky impersonated by Lawrence Tibbett just before his murder. Moussorgsky's historical music-drama first came to the Metropolitan in 1950, a magnificent spectacle in Dobujinsky's settings.

The Metropolitan Opera Guild

WHEN MRS. AUGUST BELMONT founded The Metropolitan Opera Guild in 1935, her expressed purpose was to broaden the base of participation in support of grand opera. She had the vision to realize that a great potential army of opera lovers existed in the United States beyond the loyal band of subscribers to Metropolitan Opera. Offering definite privileges in exchange for modest membership dues, the Guild attracted over 2,000 of these enthusiasts by the time of its first general meeting. By 1939 it had developed a National Membership which has by now brought up the ranks to nearly 40,000.

STUDENT PERFORMANCES

In the spring of 1937, the Guild decided to purchase a matinee performance of *Aïda* at the Metropolitan and offer it to high school students in New York City and neighboring communities at reduced prices. In the first fourteen years of this project nearly 200,000 young people between the ages of twelve and eighteen attended performances of grand opera under Guild sponsorship.

School superintendents and supervisors of music prepare their students for the experience to come. The use of recordings, lectures and slides has been incorporated into the school curriculum. The children learn to sing the choruses and play the themes. Their tastes are noted in the choice of repertory.

The active interest of so many young people caused Mrs. Belmont to organize the Student Council of The Metropolitan Opera Guild in 1944. This link between the student group and the Metropolitan serves also to extend and focus enthusiasm. The council is formed by two representatives selected from junior and senior classes of high schools affiliated with the Guild by Group Membership and one representative selected from the top grade of junior high schools. Divided into regions for purposes of convenience: Connecticut, Westchester, New Jersey, Brooklyn, Long Island and New York City, the council elects its own regional officers. These boys and girls serve as an Executive Committee which chooses the three presiding officers of the council.

Within this framework a variety of operatic activities has come to life. Local recording sessions, radio programs, musicales and assemblies have occupied the energies of the young. Screened by local and regional auditions, promising talent has been disclosed in operatic programs. Contests in costume and scenic design have demonstrated a concern with the pictorial aspects of grand opera. Whether

Even busy orchestra players take kindly to the Guild's student audience.

The Guild does not forget the past and invited Mmes. Savage, Stueckgold, Case, Scheff, Arden, Ljungberg and Mario and Messrs. De Luca and D'Angelo to join Albanese and Tagliavini at a Traviata *benefit for the Metropolitan Opera Fund.*

the boys and girls cherish ambitions of an operatic career or turn to opera for recreation and cultural interest, they prove eager torchbearers for the art and gladly accept the assistance of music supervisors and local Guild authorities in planning and executing their opera projects.

Thus the Opera Guild is building an audience for the future.

LECTURES AND EXHIBITIONS

The Guild has preached the gospel of opera through lectures by distinguished authorities to its own members, to high school and college audiences and to the general public. It has provided well-lit score desks at the sides of the dress circle for serious music students. It has held forums at the Metropolitan Museum of Art, demonstrated operatic motion pictures at the Museum of Modern Art and co-operated with the Museum of the City of New York in commemorative exhibitions. It has shown old costumes and programs, assembled the memorabilia of the past, made colored slides of present performances and debated the possibilities of the future, constantly drawing on Metropolitan resources.

PUBLICATIONS

In sixteen years the Opera Guild has prepared, published or sponsored over twenty books on opera. From the early *Opera Primer* and *Operagrams,* the Guild soon graduated to *The Metropolitan Opera Guide*, the first book of opera stories written specifically for the radio audience. Then came a series of children's books, both on individual operas and collections. *Metropolitan Opera Annals*, a compendium of opera programs from 1883-1947 was followed by *Opera Lover's Companion*, a series of articles on the background of the standard operas. The present volume is the last in a series dealing with the Opera House itself.

Opera News, the Guild's illustrated weekly magazine, covers the national and international scene, with emphasis on the Metropolitan.

Through the generous co-operation of the broadcasting companies and sponsors, the Opera Guild has participated in the Saturday intermission programs. It has also offered its own midweek radio period, either as a commentary on the opera to be broadcast the following Saturday or as a means of presenting the less well known members of the company in more ambitious selections than would normally be assigned them.

PATRIOTIC ACTIVITIES

In World War II the Guild turned its attention to patriotic service, putting thousands of opera tickets at the disposal of service men and women on leave in New York. It collected by purchase or gift over 2,000 musical instruments and distributed them, reconditioned, to army and navy hospitals through the Red Cross. It also sent instruments and recordings to lonely station outposts.

In the post-war period, it has tried to promote international amity through service to the United Nations, inviting representatives of the General Assembly or members of the Secretariat to gala performances, putting hundreds of seats at their disposal and entertaining them at intermissions.

FOR THE METROPOLITAN

The Opera Guild's primary function is to serve Metropolitan Opera, allocating to the management a part of the dues of each of its members. Through its ticket service it secures locations conveniently for its supporting members. It has assembled and purchased portraits to embellish the Opera House. A host of contributions has each year added comfort, interest or utility to the historic building. The Guild has also collaborated in every national campaign in the course of its sixteen years. Through these efforts, as well as gifts to the reserve and production funds of the Opera Association, its financial assistance has long since passed the million-dollar mark.

Lauder Greenway, the Opera Guild's president since 1947, helps Mrs. Belmont welcome Lawrence ..Tibbett and Italo Tajo to a meeting called to discuss a Guild gala. Artists always cooperate.

89

Opera From Coast To Coast

THROUGH ITS long and honorable history the Metropolitan Opera has come more and more frequently to be hailed as a "national institution." In analyzing this title and its claim to accuracy, one is impressed by four distinct factors on which the national function of the Metropolitan is at present based: the representation of leaders from other cities on its board of directors, the origin of its artists, the use of its name, the extent of its tours and the history of its broadcasts. Some of these topics have been referred to during this summary. Others are self-evident. A brief recapitulation may point the way to the future.

AMERICAN ARTISTS

From the solitary American figure, Alwina Valleria, in the inaugural Metropolitan season of 1883-84, the American contingent of artists and conductors has grown to exactly half the company, in the season of 1949-50. Including two Canadians, the roster of artists and conductors now comprises fifty-four Americans and fifty-two foreign-born individuals, although several of the latter came to this country in infancy and have never returned to Europe.

Twenty-two states are represented in the birthplaces of the fifty-four American artists, with only thirteen claiming New York as their place of birth.

Tracing the means by which the fifty-four Americans achieved their Metropolitan contracts, one finds that twenty of them were either prize-winners or honored finalists in the Metropolitan Opera Auditions of the Air, while ten more came to the attention of the management through the contest.

Thus, quite apart from the very high percentage of American citizens within the Metropolitan roster, the claim to the title of a "national institution" is well substantiated by the actual number of native born Americans.

THE NAME: "METROPOLITAN OPERA"

In the early days of Metropolitan Opera history artists were frequently referred to as coming from La Scala or Covent Garden, favorites of Bayreuth or the Paris Opera. Earlier still they boasted of the official designation of a reigning sovereign — "Chamber-singer to the Court" or some other such regal title.

Today the proudest brevet which any artist can claim is "of the Metropolitan Opera Company." From one corner of the land to the other concerts, recitals, radio programs are advertised in this manner. Opera companies playing in the spring, summer or fall announce their casts as made up of "Metropolitan artists."

It could not be other than a feather in the cap of the Metropolitan that its title is spread across the United States and beyond the sea as synonymous with the highest standards of operatic production. An indication of its national prestige, such a title becomes increasingly valuable year by year. And the Metropolitan Opera Association is becoming increasingly insistent that its value should be protected inviolate. A tradition which has taken nearly seventy years to build deserves scrupulous safeguards if it is to serve an entire nation.

THE METROPOLITAN ON TOUR

From the first season of its existence, Metropolitan Opera has taken its performances to other cities than New York. When "Abbey's Italian Opera Company" visited eight other opera houses between its autumn and spring seasons at the Metropolitan, the tour was made under the personal initiative of Mr. Abbey. The Cincinnati flood, which the troupe encountered in February, was a hazard to the impresario and his colleagues. In spite of the terms of the day, however, we think of this tour as the precedent of a long series of contributions which have emerged from the Metropolitan to benefit the country.

Because of a warehouse fire, the records of the tours made under Walter Damrosch with the company assembled by his father have all been lost. It is remembered that they played Chicago, Boston and Philadelphia in 1885 and a year later reached St. Louis.

Alwina Valleria, first American singer at the Metropolitan, who had to find an Italian disguise for the name of Schoening.

In 1901 Homer, Sembrich, Schumann-Heink and Mapleson wore shirt-waists as Grau booked the company on tour. Sidney Homer, David Bispham and Charles Gilibert are also among the intrepid passengers.

91

Once again a "Grand Opera Company" of Abbey, Schoeffel and Grau made the grand tour from December, 1889, to March, 1890, reaching as far as Mexico City before they returned to the Metropolitan on March 24. Adding the word "Italian" to their title, these gentlemen made an impressive tournee before and after their Metropolitan season of 1891-92, introducing the de Reszkes to Chicago.

After the first season following the Metropolitan fire, the tours continued steadily, in spite of the ruinous month in Chicago in 1897. At the turn of the century they reached their maximum extent, when Maurice Grau presented *Lohengrin* in a series of one night stands in Texas in November, 1901, and charged as high as $5.00 a seat for the *Magic Flute* premiere in Chicago in 1902.

Conried kept up the good work by introducing *Parsifal* to the Middle West in 1905 and then taking the production to California, Texas, New Orleans, etc. Undiscouraged by the San Francisco earthquake and fire of 1906 he got as far as Omaha in his tour of eleven cities the following spring.

The prolonged New York season of Giulio Gatti-Casazza may account for the reduction of opera touring under his regime, although Andreas Dippel, the Administrative Manager, managed to take the company to eleven cities once more in April and May, 1910. Philadelphia during the season and Atlanta for a week in April, with an occasional visit to Boston, was the rule from 1913 to 1924, although once in Philadelphia the theatre was closed by the fuel law in January, 1918. In 1924 Cleveland and Rochester were included in the circuit, with Washington and Baltimore added to the list three years later, Richmond in 1930 and Hartford and White Plains the following year.

The regime of Edward Johnson witnessed another gradual extension in the territory covered, culminating in the spring of 1948, when sixteen cities were

Prize-winners of the Auditions of the Air celebrate with the stars. L. to r.: Kent, Ribla, Resnik, Dickey, Jagel, Hayward, Merrill, Darcy, Carter, Paulee, Kullman and Gary. In front are Guarrera, Swarthout, Brownlee, Cotlow and Bollinger, all gathered at the invitation of the sponsor.

visited in addition to the Philadelphia performances, during the regular season. A warm reception on university campuses was first experienced in Bloomington, Indiana, which set a popular precedent in April, 1942. The vast size of the Cleveland Auditorium makes it possible for the Northern Ohio Opera Association to invite some 400 neighboring cities to Metropolitan performances.

Meanwhile representatives from Atlanta, Boston, Cleveland, Dallas, Los Angeles and Philadelphia bring a national viewpoint to the Association directorate.

OPERA ON THE AIR

From Christmas Day, 1931, when the first opera, *Hänsel und Gretel,* was broadcast from the Metropolitan Opera House stage, a new audience for grand opera was developed from coast to coast. During that first season, twenty-five operatic programs were broadcast from the Metropolitan, as a sustaining program, with comments by Deems Taylor during the music and announcements by Milton Cross. Only *Hänsel und Gretel* was heard in full. Other operas were presented an act or two at a time, and not always on Saturday afternoons.

The following season, 1932-33, thirteen operas were broadcast in full, eleven more in excerpts only, while Milton Cross undertook the duties of both commentator and announcer.

A commercial sponsor was introduced in the autumn of 1933 and seventeen operas were broadcast in full on Saturday afternoons, plus the Christmas *Hänsel und Gretel,* with John B. Kennedy, the news commentator, on the program. In '34 Geraldine Farrar illustrated her intermission remarks at a small piano.

Metropolitan Opera broadcasts once more became a sustaining program in 1936, with Mr. Kennedy again as commentator and Milton Cross as announcer.

Edward Johnson, Mrs. August Belmont and the Guild's director, Mrs. Herbert Witherspoon, study the returns of the Opera Ballot which reflected the tastes of the radio audience. A band of volunteers counted and classified the returns, which helped the management to plan the season.

Marcia Davenport entered the picture in the autumn of 1936, acting as musical analyst for the programs. The year before a Metropolitan performance was broadcast from Boston, while on tour. Now a Cleveland broadcast was added with seven operas put on the air in the spring seasons of 1936 and 1937.

In December, 1937, the opera broadcasts returned to the status of a sustaining program for a three year period, during which Mr. Cross carried the major responsibilities of the intermissions. Then, in the fall of 1940, the Texas Company came into the picture as sponsor and has remained in that capacity until the present date. During 1943 and 1944 the opera was broadcast from Cleveland and Chicago, where the company played on tour. In November, 1945, the opening night *Lohengrin* was broadcast for the first time.

Another milestone was established on November 29, 1948 when the opening night *Otello* was successfully telecast, to be followed by *Der Rosenkavalier* the following autumn, witnessed by cities as far as Detroit and Chicago.

Acts from *Aïda* and *Carmen* were broadcast during the Junior Performances sponsored by The Metropolitan Opera Guild in 1940 and 1941 respectively, while on one occasion the music was incorporated into the Music Appreciation program of Walter Damrosch.

Another interesting stimulus to the radio audience was provided during the spring of 1940 when a letter-writing contest was organized on "What the Metropolitan Opera Broadcasts Mean to Me." Over 17,000 letters were received and the prize-winner from each section of the country was invited to attend the opening night of the 1940-41 season as guest of the broadcasting company.

The letters themselves provided thrilling evidence of the appreciation of a wide public. The winners included a boiler-maker, a farmer, a telephone clerk, a student, a reporter and a housewife. Their love for opera was typical of the wide range of appeal offered by so universal an art.

The development of the intermission features reached a new high level in 1945-46, when Boris Goldovsky was chosen to discuss the broadcast operas with a group of distinguished guests on a program known as Opera News on the Air. In that same year the opera ballot enabled thousands of radio listeners to participate actively in the choice of repertory for the following year.

During the first nineteen years of Metropolitan Opera broadcasting, 378 performances of 70 operas have gone on the air. *Tristan und Isolde* has been broadcast 21 times, *Aïda*, 18; *Carmen*, 17; *La Traviata*, 15.

It has been estimated that from twelve to fifteen millions have found enjoyment and inspiration from this feast of music: children and shut-ins, students and soldiers, families gathered at the breakfast table in Hawaii or driving their automobiles through the snowy New England twilight, old people in libraries, following the score as they listen, young folk, appropriating the love stories of *Tristan* and *Pelléas* for themselves, even timing their weddings to the Bridal Chorus of a broadcast *Lohengrin*.

The gold curtain of the Metropolitan Opera and what it symbolizes has brought dignity and the beauty of a great tradition to the entire land.

In the Metropolitan lobby Rudolf Bing pays tribute to a great artist, Enrico Caruso.

The Future

THE APPOINTMENT of Rudolf Bing as General Manager of the Metropolitan opens a fresh chapter of its history in the season of 1950-51. Born in Vienna and trained in Berlin, the new executive brings both financial and artistic experience from important posts in Glyndebourne, London and Edinburgh.

"To carry on the excellent work of Mr. Johnson's team," Mr. Bing has announced the elevation of Reginald Allen to the position of business administrator, with Max Rudolf as artistic administrator and Francis Robinson in charge of box office and subscription arrangements. John Gutman was introduced as general assistant in the artistic departments.

Fresh talents have been heralded in production. Verdi's *Don Carlos,* opening the season on November 6, will be staged by Margaret Webster of Shakespearian fame, conducted by Fritz Stiedry with settings and costumes by Rolf Gerard. Mr. Gerard will also design scenery and costumes for Johann Strauss' *Fledermaus,* with English lyrics by Howard Dietz, conducted by Fritz Reiner and staged by Garson Kanin. Robert Edmond Jones has been invited to design the settings for *The Flying Dutchman,* directed by Herbert Graf. Bruno Walter will return to lead noteworthy revivals of Verdi's Requiem and *Fidelio,* with Kirsten Flagstad.

Among the new artists are Delia Rigal, soprano; Boris Christoff, Gottlob Frick and Fritz Krenn, basses; Hans Hotter, baritone; Elena Nikolaidi, mezzo-soprano; Paolo Silveri, baritone; Fedora Barbieri, contralto; and Victoria De Los Angeles. Alberto Erede, conductor and Fausto Cleva, formerly of the Metropolitan staff, are awaited. Helen Traubel will sing her first *Rosenkavalier* Marschallin and Flagstad her world-famous Isolde; both sopranos to share the *Ring* Cycles.

The hoped-for revival of the Auditions of the Air promises further opportunity to young American singers while the Metropolitan offers training for the first time in the duties of an apprentice assistant conductor to a young American musician. This experiment has been made possible through a grant from the Anna E. Schoen-René Fund, made available by the New York Community Trust.

The future of Metropolitan Opera depends also on considerations more elusive than administrative or artistic personnel. It must lie in the hands of a happy family and be lodged in a practical and spacious dwelling.

As a nonprofit organization, the Metropolitan Opera Association cannot enter the United States Social Security System. Since it feels an obligation to its staff, several of whom have worked for thirty years at their posts, it has filed application for voluntary coverage under the State Unemployment Insurance law.

The Metropolitan's chief problem is budgetary. Even with crowded houses and a successful tour, the organization has had to go to the general public to make both ends meet. Financed by the 1949 campaign, the Association Board has called in specialists to make extensive studies relating to the future of the opera house. Two committees have worked with a common objective: to make possible a theatre providing seating capacity sufficient to offset the high costs of present-day operatic production without lowering the highest artistic standards.

One group has investigated locations, cost, and so forth for a new opera house. The other has scrutinized reconstruction procedures in the historic theatre on Thirty-ninth Street. Much groundwork has been accomplished. It now remains to test public reaction and support before a final choice is made.

Whatever the future of Metropolitan Opera, it cherishes one asset accountable for past greatness and present promise: the character of the men and women who serve it: directors, artists, executives, staff workers and members of the generous public. Their faith, devotion and determined effort have woven the gold of the Metropolitan Opera curtain.